TEACHER LEADERSHIP

Teacher Leadership: Improving Teaching & Learning From Inside the Classroom *is lovingly dedicated to the memory of Gene Paul Litchfield and N. C. Woolverton, Jr. and to honor the entire faculty, staff, and administration of the TEAM (Together Everyone Achieves More) School, an alternative high school in Cleburne, Texas, for providing true teacher leadership to those who need it most.*

"Greater love hath no man than this, that a man lay down his life for his friends."
John 15:13
King James Version

TEACHER LEADERSHIP

Improving
TEACHING and LEARNING
From Inside the Classroom

ELAINE L. WILMORE

Foreword by Rosemary Papalewis

CORWIN PRESS
A SAGE Publications Company
Thousand Oaks, CA 91320

For information:

Corwin Press
A Sage Publications Company
2455 Teller Road
Thousand Oaks, California 91320
www.corwinpress.com

Sage Publications Ltd.
1 Oliver's Yard
55 City Road
London EC1Y 1SP
United Kingdom

Sage Publications India Pvt. Ltd.
B 1/I 1 Mohan Cooperative
   Industrial Area
Mathura Road, New Delhi 110 044
India

Sage Publications
   Asia-Pacific Pte. Ltd.
33 Pekin Street #02-01
Far East Square
Singapore 048763

Printed in the United States of America.

Library of Congress Cataloging-in-Publication Data

Wilmore, Elaine L.
Teacher leadership: Improving teaching & learning from inside the classroom/ Elaine L. Wilmore; foreword by Rosemary Papalewis.
     p. cm.
Includes bibliographical references and index.
ISBN 978-1-4129-4904-0 (cloth)
ISBN 978-1-4129-4905-7 (pbk.)
   1. Effective teaching. 2. Educational leadership. I. Title.

LB1025.3.W52 2007
371.102—dc22   2007002111

This book is printed on acid-free paper.

07   08   09   10   11   10 9 8 7 6 5 4 3 2 1

Acquisitions Editor:	Hudson Perigo
Editorial Assistant:	Jordan Barbakow
Production Editor:	Diane S. Foster
Copy Editor:	Carol Anne Peschke
Typesetter:	C&M Digitals (P) Ltd.
Proofreader:	Andrea Martin
Indexer:	Molly Hall
Cover Designer:	Michael Dubowe
Graphic Designer:	Lisa Miller

Contents

Foreword   xi
   Rosemary Papalewis

Preface   xiii
   Acknowledgments   xiv

About the Author   xvii

1. Introduction to Teacher Leadership   1
   Teacher Leadership   2
   The Socratic Method   4
   It's Up to You   7

2. A Vision for Teacher Leadership   9
   Critical Issue: Teacher Leadership   9
   Philosophical Framework   10
      The Learning Community   11
      Development and Articulation of Vision   13
      Implementation and Stewardship of Vision   17
   Problem-Based Learning   18
      The Learning Community: Dropouts and
         Cold, Hard Cash   18
         Think About It   19
      Development and Articulation of Vision:
         You've Gotta Have a Plan   19
         Think About It   20
      Implementation and Stewardship of the Vision:
         Vision or Chaos?   20
         Think About It   21
   Conclusions   21
   It's Up to You   22
         A teacher leader can enhance systematic
            school improvement by . . .   23

3. Core Values and Moral Code:
   Ethics and Integrity for All Time   **25**
       Critical Issue: The Professional Educator's Core
          Values and Moral Code   25
       Philosophical Framework   26
          Ethics: The Established Core Values and Moral Code   27
          Integrity: Identifying Your Personal Core Values and
             Moral Code   28
          Fairness: Extending Your Core Values and Moral Code   28
          Professional Demeanor: Your Core Values and Moral
             Code for the Future   29
       Problem-Based Learning   29
          Ethics: Does This Guy Have Ethical or Mental Problems?   29
             Think About It   30
          Integrity: Put Me In, Coach!   31
             Think About It   32
          Fairness: Walking the Line   32
             Think About It   33
          Professional Demeanor: Why's Everybody Always
             Picking on Me?   34
             Think About It   35
       Conclusions   35
       It's Up to You   36
          A teacher leader can enhance systematic
             school improvement by . . .   37

4. Classroom Culture and Climate:
   It Can Make You or Break You   **39**
       Critical Issue: Classroom Culture and Climate   39
       Philosophical Framework   41
          An Ethos of Learning Expectations, Appreciation,
             and Success   41
          Mutual Trust and Respect   43
          Innovation   44
       Problem-Based Learning   45
          An Ethos of Learning Expectations, Appreciation,
             and Success: What Was I Thinking
             When I Said I Would . . . ?   45
             Think About It   46
          Mutual Trust and Respect: Twinkle, Twinkle, Little
             Star, What You Say Is What You Are   46
             Think About It   47

Innovation: If We Build It, They Will Come   48
    Think About It   49
Conclusions   49
It's Up to You   50
    A teacher leader can enhance systematic
    school improvement by . . .   50

5. Curriculum and Instruction for Today's Classrooms:
Not for the Faint of Heart   **53**
Critical Issue: Curriculum and Instruction   53
Philosophical Framework   55
    Engaging and Relevant Curriculum   55
    Developmentally Appropriate Instructional Strategies   57
    Ongoing Systematic Assessment   58
Problem-Based Learning   59
    Engaging and Relevant Curriculum: United We Stand   59
        Think About It   60
    Developmentally Appropriate Instructional Strategies:
    Never, Ever, Ever Again!   60
        Think About It   61
    Ongoing and Systematic Assessment: But He Can't Read!   61
        Think About It   62
Conclusions   62
It's Up to You   63
    A teacher leader can enhance systematic
    school improvement by . . .   64

6. Equity for All Learners: Yesterday's Classroom
Is Not Coming Back   **65**
Critical Issue: Diversity and Multiculturalism   65
Philosophical Framework   66
    Identifying and Respecting the Common Ground   67
    Accepting and Appreciating Learning and
    Societal Differences   68
    Working Together to Reach the Vision   69
Problem-Based Learning   70
    Identifying and Respecting the Common Ground:
    Choir, Band, Theater, Art, or Football?   70
        Think About It   71
    Accepting and Appreciating Learning and Societal
    Differences: "I Don't Want My Kid Reading This!"   71
        Think About It   72

Working Together to Reach the Vision:
Together We Build 73
Think About It 73
Conclusions 74
It's Up to You 74
A teacher leader can enhance systematic school
improvement by . . . 75

7. Effective Communication in Today's Schools and Society:
It's Not What You Say, It's How You Say It **77**
Critical Issue: Communication 77
Philosophical Framework 78
Active Listening Before Speaking 79
The Wonderful Power of Language 80
The Public's Basic Right to Know 81
Problem-Based Learning 82
Active Listening Before Speaking: Growing Pains 82
Think About It 83
The Wonderful Power of Language: To Communicate
or Not to Communicate? 83
Think About It 84
The Public's Basic Right to Know: Show
Choir or No Choir? 84
Think About It 85
Conclusions 86
It's Up to You 86
A teacher leader can enhance systematic school
improvement by . . . 87

8. Teacher Enhancement: If You're Standing Still,
You're Moving Backwards **89**
Critical Issue: Teacher Professional Enhancement
and Development 89
Philosophical Framework 90
Looking to Your Future Through In-Depth
Personal Assessment 91
Steps in the Elaine Wilmore "How Can I
Make It Better?" Model 93
The Intrinsic Need for Quiet, Reflection, and Recreation 95
The Role of Continuous Enhancement Through
Reading, Research, and Professional Associations 98
Problem-Based Learning 100

Looking to Your Future Through In-Depth Personal
  Assessment: Taking Time to Think About It   100
    Think About It   101
The Intrinsic Need for Quiet and Recreation:
  I've Just Got to Get Out of Here   101
    Think About It   102
The Role of Continuous Enhancement
  Through Reading, Research, and
  Professional Associations: Bring It On!   103
    Think About It   104
Conclusions   104
It's Up to You   105
    A teacher leader can enhance systematic school
      improvement by . . .   105

9. Bringing It All Together   **107**
It's Up to You   111

Recommended Reading to Enhance Teacher Leadership **113**

References   **121**

Index   **123**

Foreword

I lead because I teach.

When *teacher* is coupled with the word *leader* it recognizes the seminal role that bonds students' and teachers' lives into a community of care while acknowledging the teacher's power to make a difference.

What makes a teacher a leader? Simply stated, it is an ethos of care and the skills one needs to be an inspiration. It is the qualities found in teachers who recognize their innate power to make a difference in their students' lives, to be caring and compassionate, and to be the role model who "walks the talk," who believes all students have exceptional gifts, and who takes the time to help students find and give voice to themselves.

Leaders care about their charges. The ethic of a teacher leader is summed up in the words "I care." I will be inspiring in my teaching, friendly, humorous, interested in students' lives and the homes from which they come, brave enough to leave no stone unturned to help them achieve their full potential, and active in the community, by collaborating and sharing my talents, leading other teachers to be the best they can be, and strengthening the school's administrators through truthful dialogue.

Dr. Wilmore's *Teacher Leadership: Improving Teaching & Learning From Inside the Classroom* is long overdue. The rich focus on the critical importance of developing and acknowledging the leadership skills found in classrooms finally addresses the many teachers who enter the educational administrative and leadership credential and graduate degree programs with no intention of becoming traditional administrators, preferring to remain in the classroom. These teachers and the professors who teach them will greatly benefit from a seminal work that focuses on the teacher leader and gives those teachers the courage to stay where they are most needed, where they can truly say, "I lead because I teach."

Dr. Rosemary Papalewis
California State University, Sacramento
Professor, Educational Leadership & Policy Studies
Director, Center for Teaching and Learning
Director, Professional Education Doctorates
Stafford Faculty Fellow, the National Institute on Leadership
Disability and Students Placed at Risk, University of Vermont

Preface

Teacher Leadership: Improving Teaching & Learning From Inside the Classroom addresses the critical importance of the development of leadership skills for teachers in classrooms. In the past leadership development has focused on administrators who have been responsible for the enhancement of campus teachers. Today a growing number of teachers want to enhance their leadership capacities in a manner that will facilitate student learning. These teachers do not want to become principals, counselors, or central office administrators. They want to create change, improve student performance, and grow as professionals while remaining classroom teachers. They want to become all they can be by becoming true leaders in classrooms, among teachers, and thus to enhance learning capacities in their schools and communities. Although several books are available for administrators who want to enhance their teachers' professional development, this is the first to speak directly to teachers, using a teacher's voice and providing the leadership skills teachers need to maximize their capabilities while remaining in the classroom.

There are important reasons for increasing the capacity of classroom leadership. Never has the United States experienced such a shortage of qualified and certified teachers (N.C. University, 2004; Ng, 2003). There are many reasons for this, including low pay, pressure over mandated student testing, stress, and societal changes (Williams, 1999). The structure of the job, combined with tension and time demands, can create havoc for both new and experienced teachers. This can profoundly affect their personal and family lives and jeopardize their health and job satisfaction (Blair, 2003). Many do not survive. They take early retirement or leave education entirely. The result is that we are losing high-quality classroom leaders and experiencing a shortage of well-trained and certified teachers for today's students.

It does not have to be this way. Teachers can move from "pretty good" to "wonderful" by being given the tools necessary to systematically improve teaching and learning. This will not just improve student performance; it will also greatly increase teacher job satisfaction and decrease stress. If this is of interest to you or someone you know, the time is now for *Teacher Leadership: Improving Teaching & Learning From Inside the Classroom.*

This book is unique and timely. It is both distinctive and opportune in its approach of integrating critical and practical research on leadership and school improvement with strategies for systematic school improvement in classrooms. Though based on leadership and management theory and research, it is written in an informative yet practical, readable, interesting, insightful, and inspiring manner. The concept of teacher leadership development within and outside classrooms is based in large part on the standards and core concepts, changing expectations, and vast work of the Interstate New Teacher Assessment and Support Consortium (INTASC), National Council for the Accreditation of Teacher Education (NCATE), National Board for Professional Teaching Standards, Interstate Council of Chief School Executives, Educational Leadership Constituency Council, and National Policy Board for Educational Administration. The book is written from the perspective of the INTASC standards and the research of the other scholarly groups listed here. Its goal is to present a view of what an ideal teacher leader looks and behaves like. If we cannot first define an ideal teacher leader, how can we make progress toward becoming one? Therefore, this book presents the concept of the ideal teacher leader who seeks to be and do everything realistically possible to improve the lives of children, one child at a time. Anything less is less than what our children, our society, and our future deserve. So read on. Then go make a difference with each child you meet. The reward will come not just from those you know you have helped. It will also come from those who were the most trying, who got on your nerves the most, and who created total havoc, because you will know you influenced how their lives could someday be. For this your effort will reap true, if sometimes silent, rewards.

ACKNOWLEDGMENTS

My life is blessed beyond all reasonable measure. First, my precious family and friends love and support me even when my ideas create havoc in their lives. These include Greg, Brandon, Brooke, Brenda, Ben, Samuel, Matthew, Sarah, Sophie, Zachary, T. N., Ella, Jeff, and Larry Wilmore, Brittani and Ryan Rollen, Bill and Marlene Carter, Wes and Helen Nelson, Dr. Joe and Kathy Martin, Larry and Jo Nell Jones, Dr. Wade, Renae, and Emily Smith, Rev. Robert A. and JoAnn Graham, Dr. Linda and

Ron Townzen, and precious lifelong friends Melda Cole Ward and Kerry Van Doren Pedigo. My church family, the Field Street Baptist Church, likewise stands beside me and calls me their own. We must all express our appreciation to the Educational Leadership Constituent Council, Association for Supervision and Curriculum Development, National Council for the Accreditation of Teacher Education, Interstate School Leaders Licensure Consortium, Texas State Board for Educator Certification, American Association of School Administrators, National Association of Secondary School Principals, National Association of Elementary School Principals, and other groups for their vast research on leadership development.

I am particularly blessed to teach in and lead the M.Ed. in educational leadership program at Dallas Baptist University in Dallas, Texas, otherwise known as my personal "Heaven on the Hill." Thank you to visionary leaders President Dr. Gary Cook, Provost Dr. Gail Linam, Dr. Denny Dowd, Dr. Chuck Carona, Dr. Rick Gregory, Kee Badders, Paula Moresco, and Regina McNair for maintaining your faith in me as you simultaneously roll your eyes at the things I say or do.

Last, I could not be anything but for the grace and mercy of my Lord and Savior, Jesus Christ, who leads me beside the still waters every day of my life.

Corwin Press gratefully acknowledges the contributions of the following individuals:

Carmen Bourg Riedlinger, PhD
Chair of Graduate Education
Our Lady of Holy Cross College
New Orleans, LA

Gilberto Arriaza
Professor, Educational Leadership Dept.
San Jose State University
San Jose, CA

Thomas C. McGuire
Education Dept. Chair
University of La Verne
La Verne, CA

About the Author

 **Elaine L. Wilmore,** PhD, is a professor and director of the educational leadership program and the assistant vice president for educational networking at Dallas Baptist University in Dallas, Texas. She is also writer-in-residence at the historic Ingleside Bed and Breakfast in Brenham, Texas. She has served as special assistant to the dean for NCATE accreditation and associate professor of educational leadership and policy studies at the University of Texas at Arlington (UTA), president of the National Council of Professors of Educational Administration, president of the Texas Council of Professors of Educational Leadership, and president of the Board of Trustees of the Cleburne Independent School District, where she continues to serve. She is the founding director of school administration programs, Educational Leadership UTA, and the Scholars of Practice Program at UTA, where she was principal investigator for multiple grants for innovative field-based principal preparation programs. She has served as chair of educational administration and director of university program development at UTA, where she also developed and was the original chair of the Faculty Governance Committee for the College of Education.

Dr. Wilmore is and has been active on many local, state, and national boards. These include the Executive Committee of the National Council of Professors of Educational Administration, the American Educational Research Association Executive Committee on the Teaching in Educational Administration SIG, the Texas Principals Leadership Initiative, and the Texas Consortium of Colleges of Teacher Education, and she has served as a program and folio reviewer for the Educational Leadership Constituent Council. She holds the distinction of being among the very few who have served as both a private school and public school district board of trustees member.

Dr. Wilmore was a public school teacher, counselor, and elementary and middle school principal before she moved to higher education. In addition to her significant work in educational leadership and innovative program development, she enjoys reading, writing, walking, music, spending time with those she loves, and anything chocolate. She is married to Greg Wilmore and the mother of three wonderful children, Brandon and Brooke Wilmore and Brittani Rollen, a fabulous son-in-law, Ryan Rollen, two outstanding pugs named Lacianna "Lacie" and Annabella Rose, and a 19-year-old cat named Yum. She misses her parents, Lee and Irene Litchfield, who are in Heaven, and seeks to honor their memory through the way she lives her life.

Introduction to Teacher Leadership

"Delegating work works, provided the one delegating works, too."

—Robert Half

Leadership is a strange topic that defies simple explanations. There are leaders in every type of organization, from businesses to schools to nations. Most of the time when we think of school leaders we think of superintendents, principals, or other people in positions of authority. Conversely, teachers sometimes are considered the organizational worker bees, or followers of the sage direction provided by others. Staff development for teachers usually is centered on instructional or academic topics, whereas administrator development often addresses issues related to the elusive topic of leadership.

But are not teachers leaders also? If teachers do not lead and guide students in their classrooms and in the cocurricular and extracurricular activities they sponsor, who does? Inside classrooms teachers lead students toward academic success, which will help them to lead better lives, with better families and careers. The ultimate goal is to affect society as a whole. Usually, the higher the educational level, the greater the impact on a range of fields, from economics to the arts.

Yet where is the concept of teachers as leaders of classrooms, schools, gymnasiums, theaters, studios, and so on addressed? Although teachers are routinely urged to improve their instructional and academic skills, where is the cry for improving teacher leadership skills? Does it not make sense that as teachers improve these skills, they will simultaneously

Figure 1.1   Teacher Leadership

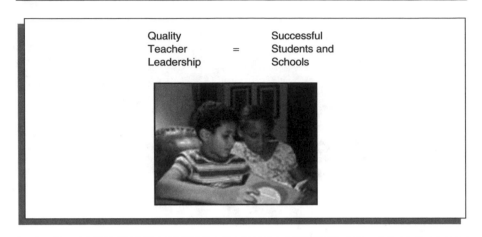

Source: Photo reprinted with permission from Kimberly Miller.

improve other aspects of their personal, academic, and community lives? Developing high-quality teachers into teacher leaders will affect the success of both students and schools (Figure 1.1).

TEACHER LEADERSHIP

As early as 1992, Peter Strodl was developing a conceptual framework to identify the existence of teacher leadership skills. His work showed that greater teacher participation in decision making improved instructional leadership in classrooms. His model included three major themes:

- Potential for informal leadership
- Identification of problems and conflicts
- Empowerment of teachers to work toward their solutions

His research showed that more than one leader is necessary for schools to thrive. Therefore, informal teacher leaders who work from a group ethic and value system are essential.

Keith Joseph Suranna and Laura-Eve Moss (1999) studied preservice teacher perceptions of the role of the teacher leader. Approximately half thought it was important for teachers and principals to share leadership capacities. They thought that with time and seasoning teachers could become leaders and change agents in their campuses and districts. Suranna (2000) also studied a 5-year teacher preparation program at the University of Connecticut. The study revealed a significant gap in the research regarding the extent to which preservice teacher education facilitates teacher leadership. A teacher leader was perceived to be a good classroom teacher who was current in theory and best practice and who held students to high expectations while also providing consistent care and support. Teacher leaders were perceived to work in partnership with their principals on their own and their colleagues' professional development. Teacher leaders were seen as those who were willing to stand up to obstacles that could prevent them or their colleagues from doing their best. They identified teacher leadership characteristics as including high-quality teaching, student academic and social developmental support, and encouragement for colleagues on specific tasks. These tasks included attending meetings and conferences when others were unable to attend, taking notes, providing helpful suggestions and positive feedback, and actively listening.

Continuing to work together, Suranna and Moss (2002) explored teacher leadership in the context of teacher preparation. They found teacher leaders to be good classroom instructors who were committed to the lives of their students, were engaged in curriculum development, acted as change agents through involvement in school and district committees, and, when necessary, challenged others to strive for their best for the benefit of schools and students. Their work showed that for teacher leadership to thrive, teachers must collaborate with others, including their principals.

In 2001 Mary Ellen Krisko developed a survey to identify characteristics of teacher leaders. She found eight common traits: These teachers are creative, flexible, and lifelong learners; in addition, they enjoy humor, are efficacious, are willing to take risks, and have good intrapersonal and interpersonal skills. Teachers identified as having these characteristics were determined to be capable of developing leadership capacity to initiate change in an effective learning community.

Richardson Ackerman and Sarah Mackenzie (2006) identified the characteristics and responsibilities of teacher leaders. They found that although formal roles for teacher leaders do still exist, as in the earlier findings of Krisko, the new role of teacher leaders today is more informal and gained from classroom experience. Teacher leaders implement these informal roles in such ways as sharing their own classroom practices and personal expertise, mentoring new educators, asking probing questions, and modeling collaboration. They care about their students and the discrepancy that often exists between the school's mission, or ideal, and actual practice. Therefore, teacher leaders can be seen as the school's conscience. They can also be seen as threatening to administrators and colleagues who view them as potentially upsetting the status quo.

These are not the only authors to note the importance of developing leadership capacity from within. Other books, from Roland Barth's *Improving Schools From Within* (1991) to Michael Fullan's *The New Meaning of Educational Change* (2001), cover a decade of work addressing the issue. Judith Warren Little (1985) addressed the emerging role of leadership development for teachers. Joseph Murphy (2005) and David Paul Hook (2006) made the connection between teacher leadership and school improvement. Then Gayle Moller and Anita Pankake (2006) urged principals to share leadership by leading with them instead of being subservient under them. Sandra Harris (2005) identified specific strategies and roles teachers can use to build relationships to improve student performance.

So the time is ripe for classroom teachers to rise, learn, and be heard but to do so in a way that is nurturing and collaborative rather than threatening. One model by which this can be accomplished is that of servant leadership. This model was first popularized by the work of Robert Greenleaf (1982, 1991). By becoming servants to others, teachers seek to avoid intimidating them, addressing Ackerman and Mackenzie's (2006) concerns. In few professions or vocations is servant leadership more profoundly needed or used than in education today as teachers seek to serve students, families, and communities. In so doing, teacher leaders seek to develop and sustain learning communities where groups collaborate, grow, and thrive as they work together toward a common goal or vision (Glaser, 2004; Murphy, Beck, Crawford, Hodges, & McGaughy, 2001; Patrikakou, Weissberg, Redding, & Walberg, 2005; Roberts & Pruitt, 2003; Rubin, 2002; Sullivan & Glanz, 2005).

THE SOCRATIC METHOD

Ancient Greek philosopher Socrates lived from 470 to 399 B.C.E. in and around Athens. He is largely thought to be the founder of Western philosophy as we know it today. Socrates rarely used the stand-and-deliver direct instructional approach so common in modern classrooms. Rather, he taught through discovery by using probing questions, forcing students to learn to think critically to draw conclusions, become more self-aware, provide generalizations, and solve problems. He thought the self-discovery process was of more long-term benefit than direct instruction and that it would produce a deeper level of thought and application (Palincsar & Brown, 1984).

A Socratic approach to how teachers can be servant leaders to the learning community through the core issues of vision, ethics, curriculum and instruction, equity, communication skills, and teacher enhancement is used herein. Socrates himself used three main components in his teaching: systematic questioning, inductive reasoning, and universal definitions. The primary component we will use is the systematic questioning approach, through which you will learn to apply open-ended questions when confronted with problems (Overholser, 1992). In the Socratic method, questions are designed to help you think critically. Socrates stressed that all answers to truth lie within us. Thus, in our efforts to become true teacher leaders, the truth lies within us. Do not accept the first response that comes to mind. Dig deeper, for that is where the substance of reflection lies. Your growth as a teacher leader will be directly proportionate to the amount of time and effort you put into it.

Socrates required his students to do an in-depth search for truth. Should we not do at least as much as the ancient Greeks? If you give only cursory attention to the information presented in this book, if you provide only simplistic responses to the questions, you will not have put much effort into it. Socrates would not have allowed that. However, if you dig deep into your heart and mind to stretch yourself, to analyze and respond from every part of your soul, you will be surprised at the growth you will experience.

After each case study presented in this book and at the end of each chapter, there are open-ended questions that use the Socratic method. Case studies sometimes do not tell you exactly how the situation ends. Questions are designed for you to dig deep, think critically, and use an inductive method of defining your response to the concepts presented. In this manner you will be actively participating in self-discovery as you learn about teacher leadership roles and responsibilities. The content is presented from an idealistic point of view as we learn together how to exercise the knowledge, skills, and dispositions called for by the Interstate New Teacher Assessment and Support Consortium, National Board for Professional Teaching Standards, National Council for Accreditation of Teacher Education, and various state certification examinations such as the Texas Examinations of Educator Standards.

In our efforts to develop and implement teacher leadership skills, we are focusing our attention on six critical issues:

- Vision
  - If we don't know where we want to be as teacher leaders, how will we know when we get there?
- Ethics and Integrity
  - Just because something is legal does not necessarily mean it is the right thing for teachers as leaders to do.

- Curriculum and Instruction
  - Curriculum is what we teach. Instruction is how we teach it. Together they are the meat and potatoes of what education and teacher leadership are all about.
- Equity for All Learners
  - Just because an instructional strategy has worked in the past does not necessarily mean it is appropriate for all learners in today's increasingly diverse society. We must meet the challenge of addressing the needs of every student.
- Effective Communication Skills
  - We can be the smartest people ever to have lived, but if we can't communicate effectively and motivate our students, then our vast intelligence or abundant academic knowledge does not mean a thing.
- Teacher Enhancement
  - If we are not growing, we are standing still while the world surges ahead. The gap between our knowledge, skills, and dispositions and the ever-changing needs of students continues to widen. Consequently, by standing still we are moving backwards. Leaders do not move backwards. They march forward. How can we as teachers march forward to improve ourselves as educators and human beings for now and the future?

There has been no better time in history than now for masses of teachers to step to the leadership plate and demand the respect they deserve as the professionals they are. This is true for all teachers, whether they be in public or private schools. Until we are satisfied with the learning and achievement of every student in the land, our job is not complete. It will never be complete until people in all families, of all countries, races, and abilities, have a solid quality of life in which the basics of food, clothing, and shelter are addressed. For diverse cultures to be successful and work together in harmony, all citizens must be able to read, write, and communicate effectively. Politicians everywhere give lip service to these issues, but it is often up to teachers to get the job done.

So do you want to become this kind of teacher leader? Do you want to be a part of changing society on the most basic level? Come along as we journey into your future to enhance your skills and make you the greatest teacher leader you can possibly be. Most answers lie in the depths of our hearts, minds, and souls. Come along on our journey as we seek to improve society and schools today from within classrooms. Let's start with your classroom first.

IT'S UP TO YOU

1. What calls educators to become teacher leaders? Why would an overworked, underpaid educator want to take this additional giant step in time, commitment, and effort?

2. Although much research has been done in both business and educational realms, there is still a lack of commonly accepted leadership standards. How does this absence influence changing expectations of student performance in a changing multicultural society?

3. How do teacher leaders' roles and responsibilities compare with those of principals, superintendents, and politicians?

4. Recognition and appreciation often are positive motivators. What types of recognition or appreciation do teacher leaders get, if any? Are they necessary to encourage or produce teacher leaders?

5. What types of influence do teacher leaders have in their schools and communities? On political and national issues?

6. Describe specific ways a teacher leader can use servant leadership to improve student learning and well-being in the classroom.

A Vision for Teacher Leadership

CRITICAL ISSUE: TEACHER LEADERSHIP

King David is a beloved legendary hero of the Jewish people from historic times before the birth of Christ. Whether you believe his reign to be fact, fiction, or myth, most people have heard the story of the teenaged David killing the giant Goliath with a single stone and slingshot. David had a vision. Others, including King Saul, who was ruler at the time, wrung their hands in worry over how the small Israelite army could possibly take on the huge and better-equipped invaders. Yet David, although still a boy, killed the giant. No one else had the fortitude to battle Goliath because they feared certain death. Even Saul would not fight the giant. But young David did exactly that. Saul was overjoyed when David volunteered. He even offered David his own armor. But David refused. He refused fancy weapons also. David was determined to kill Goliath and free his people from oppression using a basic tool of his trade as a shepherd: a slingshot. He was not planning to do this for any personal fame or prosperity. He was doing it because he felt a special calling, his vision, to get rid of the huge egomaniac who was tormenting his people.

So David, armed only with the slingshot he used to protect his sheep, bent to the ground and selected the best smooth stone he could find. During this time Goliath continued to taunt both him and the entire Israelite army.

Goliath, seeing David was still a teenager, jeered about David's youth, inexperience, and lack of appropriate armor and equipment. Besides being a physical giant, Goliath was a bully. Yes, they had bullies even back then.

Yet David was not deterred. He had a vision of what was to be done. Absolutely nothing, not even a big-mouthed giant, was going to stop him from doing what he felt called to do. So while Goliath continued to harass, David set the stone in his slingshot, pulled back, and let loose.

The perfectly shot stone hit Goliath squarely on the forehead and killed him on the spot. That was the end of the big-mouthed giant. He was dead. Goliath's invading tribe ran to the hills to escape the jubilant Jews and their young hero. Because David was true to his vision of what needed to happen, he did not let the prospect of death stop him. He killed Goliath with one shot. Goliath's army rapidly retreated while David's empowered people sang songs of triumph and delight.

There are lessons to be learned from this teenager with a slingshot. There were many obvious reasons for David not to fight Goliath. After all, no one else wanted to. David was young. He was a shepherd, not a warrior. He had no military training. But he did have a calling. Instead of surrendering to all the reasons not to fulfill his mission, he stepped forward, set his eyes on Goliath, acted on faith, and shot the stone that saved his people. By remaining true to his vision, David changed the course of history. He remains a beloved Jewish hero to this day.

The same needs for a calling and commitment to a vision are evident in the school learning community today. It is easy to blame others for student learning that is less than ideal. Yet remember that David did not have an ideal situation either. But he didn't give up. He remained committed to solving the problem.

PHILOSOPHICAL FRAMEWORK

Vision is what everything we do, or ever hope to be, is all about. It is not where we are right now. It is where we hope to be someday. It is not what our students are achieving now. It is what we want them to achieve. Without vision, we are nothing.

This is particularly true in our lives as teacher leaders. We must first identify where we want to be before we can plan exactly what we must do to get us there. This is true in our personal as well as our professional lives. Therefore, if we are committed to having more quiet time for ourselves and time with our families, then that is our vision. If we want to become healthier, that becomes our vision. But if we do not have a plan for exactly what we will do to become healthier and a specific timeline for implementing it, then we do not have a vision. We have a dream.

If we want every student to have basic literacy skills, we cannot just hope that it will suddenly happen this year. We must have a plan to guarantee that it will take place. A vision means nothing if we do not have a plan for how to achieve it. As Stephen Covey (1990) says, we must begin with the end in mind. We must know where we want to go or what we want to achieve as teacher leaders and in our personal lives.

Then we need to develop a plan and a timeline to turn our vision into reality. Create the plan, then work the plan:

- First, identify what your vision is and whether it is personal or professional.
- Then, very strategically, identify the exact things that need to occur for your vision to be achieved.
- Next, identify the resources, including time, you will need to help you achieve your vision.
- Then choose your timeline for success. How will you know you are making progress in a timely manner?
- Last, decide how you will evaluate your plan's success. Remember, what gets measured gets done.

All of this may sound simplistic, but done right, it is not. There wasn't anything easy about the way Socrates taught. This method takes intense reflection, analysis, and, introspection. It takes foresight and planning. It takes resources and time management. Are you ready to make this commitment? If so, read on.

The Learning Community

Before teachers can become leaders in the learning community, we must define what a learning community is. A learning community is a group of people who work closely together, always striving forward, toward collaboratively developed goals. In schools learning communities work in groups and use effective communication and team processes to achieve their common goals. They may initiate study groups that will enhance the learning community. They provide learning opportunities for teachers and others through classroom observations, mentoring, and other collaborative and cooperative strategies to enhance student learning. Some use portfolios to document their progress toward their goals. All work hard to sustain and nurture the learning community as a thriving, alive entity focused on change for the sake of improvement rather than change for the sake of change (Murphy, 2005; Roberts & Pruitt, 2003; Sullivan & Glanz, 2005).

A learning community can consist of more than teachers and principals. It can include staff, support personnel, and central office administrators. It is important to discern that the learning community is more than the people involved. It is focused on the growth and learning that must be occurring. Learning communities must work closely together so members can make intelligent and informed choices on all issues. These groups can also be both internal and external to a specific school. Teachers from across the district can join together to study a specific issue, such as block scheduling or targeted reading programs. Teachers from within a certain campus can also meet to study the same or different issues. The main characteristic of a learning community is that it is a growing, dynamic group of individuals committed to learning about a common issue or problem or to improving relationships to increase effectiveness. Thus, a hospital emergency room could be defined as a part of a learning community because each group of medical practitioners has its own role, but they function together for the benefit of patients.

Effective learning communities in schools

- Increase learning and achievement
- Increase student self-efficacy and confidence
- Conduct collaborative discussions and decision making
- Have commonly developed goals and strategies to reach them
- Improve alignment of curriculum, instruction, and assessment
- Have teachers committed to being lifelong learners
- Foster an innovative, nurturing environment

So what does the learning community have to do with teachers as leaders in classrooms? It is up to teachers as leaders to take a bold, proactive stand in communicating the vision, mission, and goals of the school to anyone who will listen. This may occur internally, at parent conferences, at Parent-Teacher Association (PTA) or Parent-Teacher Organization (PTO) meetings, in the hallway, in the cafeteria, or anywhere else. But none of us can stop there. Teacher leaders are actively involved in articulating the campus vision everywhere they go. This includes in their neighborhoods, in community organizations, and even at the local store. Teacher leaders work hard to articulate the vision of the school without ceasing, wherever they are, and in whatever circumstances they find themselves. They articulate advocacy for children of all ages at all times. They speak up about the importance of a free and appropriate education for every child in a democratic society.

Teacher leaders also focus on the importance of education for our nation, our future as a people, and the legacy by which we will someday be judged. All of this takes place regularly as all of us work together to spread the word of the school vision, mission, and goals and why they are

Figure 2.1   Vision and Goal-Setting Alignment

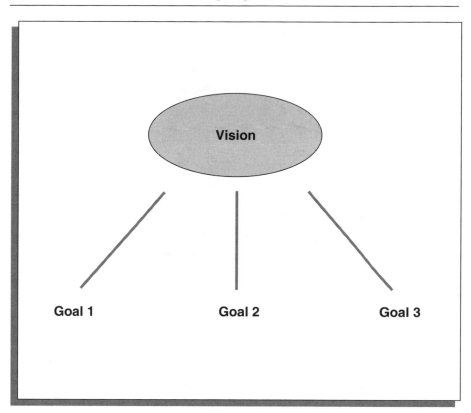

important. Teacher leaders encourage others to be valiant workers for all children regardless of their circumstances. In this way the learning community matures, has organizational ownership of campus goals and plans, and grows in knowledge and commitment to the needs of the school and district. Everyone in the learning community encourages and solicits others in the cause of a solid education for every student, both today and tomorrow.

Development and Articulation of Vision

As shown in Figure 2.1, in order for a vision of student, classroom, and campus success to become a reality, it first needs to be developed and articulated so that every person in the learning community understands what it is, why it is important, what is needed to achieve it, and what his or her role is in making it happen. How the vision is developed is central to its success. It cannot be done by administrators alone, or even a small group of teachers, who decide what should be done or how it should be done. Conversely, for a vision or anything else to be successful, it must have commitment from those involved. That means that determining the school vision is a time-intensive process that cannot be done in one brief session. Instead, it must be developed over time with significant, truthful, and insightful input from multiple constituencies in the learning community. Everyone may not agree on every issue involved. That is not unusual. Start on the areas in which most people do agree and work outward from there.

There are multiple models for consensus building, but the easiest is to ask everyone to come with an open mind, to listen actively to diverse perspectives, and to not block an idea because it is something that is new, foreign, or outside their comfort zone. We once had a leader who said the seven last words of a dying organization are, "We never did it that way before." That is true for any organization. Schools are vibrant, living, growing units that should be willing to look at everything being done with fresh perspectives. Teacher leaders take a proactive stance, constantly seeking ways to improve everything they do to maximize student learning and critical thinking skills. If we keep on doing what we have always done, we will keep on getting what we have always gotten—or even less in our changing global society.

Another reason to involve multiple stakeholders is that people support what they help create. If teachers from different grade or content areas have vastly different views on appropriate instructional strategies, those are the exact teachers who need to be involved in developing the mission. Later they should be an integral part of creating consensus on exactly how to get the school or classroom from where it is now, otherwise known as reality, to where it needs to be, otherwise known as the vision. Reaching a consensus does not mean that everyone agrees on everything all the time. It is a part of critical analysis to seriously look at all issues from various points of view. However, reaching a consensus does mean that a position is reached that most of the organization can support. By analyzing various forms of data, teacher leaders and other staff members achieve a realistic understanding of the current reality of the campus or classroom. It may be good, bad, or ugly, but it is where we are. The vision goes way beyond reality to where you want your school or classroom to be. Data-driven decision making focuses on making decisions based on current realities and facts rather than perceptions. Making proactive decisions based on data results in forward motion and greater student learning and productivity.

- What are the things you want your students to know, be able to do, and be known for when they leave your campus? (This is not just a high school issue. You may be a teacher leader in a preschool campus. These strategies apply to everyone.)

Figure 2.2 Creating an Action Plan to Reach the Campus or Classroom Vision

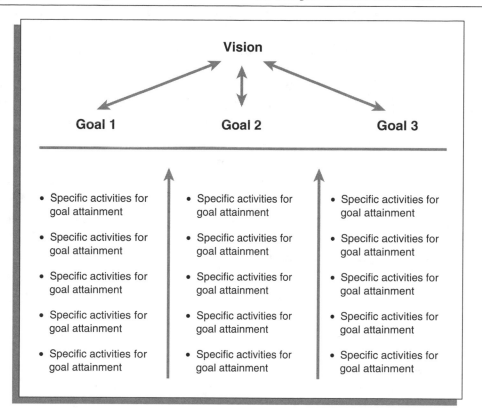

• What kinds of citizenship skills do you want them to have or be developing?

• Exactly what needs to be done, by whom, and with what resources, to promote your students' knowledge, skills, and dispositions from where they are today to the collective vision of where you want them to be?

When you can answer all of those tough questions, you will have identified your campus and classroom vision and a strategic plan that details what must be done to accomplish it (Figure 2.2).

That does not mean it will be easy. Few things in life that are worthwhile are ever easy. In the 2006 Winter Olympics, it would have been easy for Sasha Cohen to give up after she fell twice in the long program of the women's figure skating finals. That would have been the easy thing: Just finish the skate, go home, hide, and cry. But that is not what Sasha did. With much of the world watching, she pulled from her innermost self to find the character, fortitude, and perseverance she needed to pull herself together and finish the long program with the grace, poise, and elegance she is known for. Sasha did not take the easy way out, and neither should we. By a combination of mini-miracles she ended up with the silver medal, which she promptly and humbly called a gift.

As teacher leaders you can never give up, even when you want to go home, hide, or cry. There will always be days when you wish you could. But to dig deep within yourself in the darkest circumstances and still end up a winner for students takes true grit. That is what being a teacher leader is really about. Not all teachers are cut out for it. Are you?

After the vision has been collaboratively developed, the next step is to articulate it in a clear and strong manner. A leader cannot blow an uncertain trumpet. You are your classroom's trumpeter, and you are playing this one as a solo. That means you cannot rely on anyone else to articulate, communicate, or market the vision of your school or your classroom. The buck stops with you. It is up to you to articulate the vision to anyone and everyone in the learning community, whether they think they are interested or not. Nothing builds support like enthusiasm. As a teacher leader you are a cheerleader for your school and campus, whether you ever thought of yourself in those terms or not.

You may be thinking that you are not cut out to be a cheerleader. You may be a quiet, behind-the-scenes leader who is detail oriented and very good at pulling all the pieces together quietly. There is absolutely nothing wrong with that. Society needs teacher leaders with strengths in every area. The key is having commitment to the cause of achieving the mission for every student, never giving up on anyone or anything, expecting the best from everyone and especially those who are struggling, and, often, having higher expectations for each student than they have for themselves. It is amazing how high someone can soar when they have someone cheering them on, lifting them up, and believing in them. Think about it. Has there ever been someone in your life who has encouraged you to dream big dreams and believed wholeheartedly that you would achieve them? How did that make you feel? Really reflect on that. Chances are that it made you feel very good. Chances are that someone else's faith in your abilities did wonderful things for your motivation and confidence. Our goal can be to be that person in as many ways as possible for others.

Go be that someone for someone today. Do it again tomorrow, and the next day, and the next. Never stop. The reward for your efforts will come back to you in the future society you are helping to create as you teach others to dream really big dreams each day of their lives. From dreams come productivity, creativity, and critical analysis skills as they change from elusive, hopeful concepts to practical, implemented ideas that improve student performance.

Implementation and Stewardship of Vision

Once a vision has been identified and articulated, it is time to put it into action. In some ways implementing the vision is easier than developing and articulating it, but in others it is much harder. The distinction is in the kind of person you are. Some people are better than others at seeing the big picture of the vision. Others are better at communicating what you are trying to do and explaining why it is important so that others can understand it. Then there are some who are better at putting the whole thing into practice. It can be compared to the difference between creating a design for a house and actually pouring the concrete, doing the electrical wiring, installing the plumbing, and so on to build it. Some people are developers. Others are implementers. Both are necessary, whether they are designing and building a house or developing and implementing a campus vision.

Back when we were talking about collaboratively developing a vision, we also talked about identifying the things that need to happen and the resources that are necessary for achieving the vision. At this point, those are the things teacher leaders do. We previously developed the plan. Now teacher leaders implement it. Sasha Cohen ended up with the silver medal after falling twice even though it would have been easy to give up. She did not let terrible obstacles get the best of her. She stuck with the rest of her plan even under difficult circumstances.

Her chief competitor, Irina Slutskaya, may have thought that she had the gold medal wrapped up after Sasha fell twice. But, for whatever reason, she did not work her plan. Perhaps this was her own idea, or perhaps she deviated at the direction of her coach. Regardless, she skated conservatively, took no risks, and managed to fall herself. Because she did not take any risks and still fell, the judges were not able to award her as many points for the level of difficulty of her performance. Therefore, Sasha took the silver and Irina ended up with the bronze. The difference between the two skaters could be that Sasha displayed more inner fortitude and stuck with her plan. She was a steward of her vision, her plan, even when she was stressed and performing in front of a worldwide television audience. Irina did not. The color of their respective medals tells the rest of the story.

The same is true for teacher leaders. The time is now for developing, implementing, and nurturing a plan that is more proactive than we have seen in the past. It is a time to make research-based change by stepping out of our comfort zones and trying new ways to improve student learning. Will this involve risks? Yes, it will. Will every new strategy we try be successful? No, it will not. But we will never know what we can achieve if we are not willing to take risks, challenge preconceived ideas, be trustworthy stewards of the vision, and go for the gold for every student.

PROBLEM-BASED LEARNING

The Learning Community:
Dropouts and Cold, Hard Cash

As a vocational teacher at A. H. Wheat High School, Santos Gonzalez was highly concerned about the dropout rate of Hispanic students. Many of the students were first-generation high school students with limited English proficiency. Many of them struggled academically. Santos, who was bilingual, was happy to have many of these students in his program. He was acutely aware that the school had an unacceptable percentage of Hispanic dropouts. Because he could speak Spanish, Santos spent many hours talking with the students, encouraging them to stay in school and counseling them about the importance of a high school diploma for their future earning capability and success in life.

However, to teenagers with strong family ties and meager means, the prospect of bringing in immediate extra money from low-paying jobs at a local plant was enticing. As adolescents, they had difficulty seeing beyond the immediacy of cash in hand to the greater earnings after graduation. They saw school as a hassle that got in the way of bringing home money. Cash in their pockets was more lucrative than Shakespeare. Even with Santos regularly reinforcing the need for an education and the work skills they were learning in his program, it was still tough for the students to resist the lure of cold, hard cash.

A major part of the A. D. Wheat High School vision was to reduce the dropout rate and increase the graduation rate of Hispanic students. Santos believed in this mission. He also had the foresight to see that students would not stop quitting school to go to work unless an intervention took place. As a vocational teacher who knew the students well and who also spoke Spanish, Santos made an appointment with several officials at the local plant that was hiring many of his students. He explained what was happening and asked them to help by not hiring the teens until after they graduated.

Although Santos thought it would probably be a useless trip, he was pleasantly surprised. His visit was well received and resulted in subsequent meetings that included more plant officials, the high school principal, and others interested in the long-term success of the students. Together they sought to create a plan that would be mutually beneficial to the students, the school, and the plant. In addition, collegiality and collaboration between the two entities increased significantly. Although change did not occur overnight, initial steps to reduce the dropout rate were implemented.

Think About It

1. In what ways did Santos demonstrate teacher leadership skills in his learning community? In what ways did he fail to do so?

2. Santos sought to decrease the Hispanic dropout rate while increasing the graduation percentages through collaboration and teamwork. Beyond these initial steps, what else could he do to accomplish the same goals?

3. Describe other teacher leadership strategies that educators in math, English, science, and social studies could use to achieve the campus vision.

4. Compare and contrast the appropriateness of teachers as leaders in making initial contact with the plant with the appropriateness of campus or district administrators making the initial contact.

5. In what ways could the problem of student dropouts be better communicated and addressed with parents for problem solving within the learning community?

6. It is often difficult to communicate with parents who do not speak English or have limited English proficiency. What are some ways teacher leaders could exercise creativity in addressing this complex problem?

Development and Articulation of Vision: You've Gotta Have a Plan

The voters of Winter Park Consolidated School District narrowly defeated a bond election for constructing new schools and renovating others. Various factors were involved in the defeat, including some people who opposed increasing taxes and others who did not want to see the closure of several schools that were more than 100 years old because of their historical significance in the community.

Winter Park now has an opportunity to obtain substantial state funding that can be used only for new school construction. But there is a catch. The state will issue the funds based on a minimum of matching funds from the district. This would have worked fine if the original bond issue had passed. Because it did not, the district has no money with which to match the state grant. Winter Park faces the difficult decision of whether to call for another bond election so soon after the original or to let the opportunity for the state funds go by without application.

Think About It

1. In what ways can teachers as leaders help in the decision making, development, and articulation of a vision to address this complex problem?

2. How does developing and articulating a cohesive vision for district facilities affect teachers as leaders of classrooms?

3. In what ways could teachers enhance their leadership skills while working within the district as an integral part of the decision-making process?

4. In what ways could teachers serve as leaders in determining why the first bond election did not pass and documenting ways to address these problems so they will not recur if the district decides to call for a second bond election?

5. How can teachers help articulate and substantiate the need for improved school facilities in the school community?

6. Is this a teacher leadership issue? Why or why not?

Implementation and Stewardship of the Vision: Vision or Chaos?

The vision of Charles Carona Middle School included having every student pass difficult annual state-mandated tests. Plans to accomplish this goal were cooperatively developed and clearly articulated to the entire learning community. There were significant parental, faculty, and staff input and support for the development of the vision.

At first, the faculty and parents responded in a positive manner. Teachers began to put more attention into their lesson plans and their instructional methods. Parents thought of ways they could assist their children at home. Likewise, the students increased their focus. They understood the importance of the state exams.

As the spring semester rolled on and test dates got closer, the math department head, Paris Marcum, became increasingly anxious about how the students would do on the math portion of the test. The more stressed Paris got, the more pressure she put on everyone else. However, she did all of this in the name of ensuring the implementation and attainment of the campus vision.

But as time went by, Paris's anxiety seemed to get the best of her. She kept intense pressure on the teachers, who ultimately began to resent it. They felt that the constant pressure was interfering with the students' academic and developmental processes. The teachers were greatly concerned that putting too much pressure on the students was detrimental and that students were shutting down and not learning anything at all.

When the teachers tried to address this concern with Paris, she did not respond well. Regardless of what the teachers said, Paris kept returning to the importance of the tests and the pressure she was under from administration to guarantee good math scores, and she said that everyone needed to keep the pressure on the students and, if necessary, increase it. She stressed that it would not be good for any of them to have to explain to campus administrators why the students did not do well on the math portion of the tests. From Paris's perspective, she was standing firm in support of the campus vision of academic excellence. From the rest of the math teachers' perspectives, she was out of control. Each saw the same issue through vastly different eyes.

Think About It

1. How could the math leaders have communicated effectively to Paris that the pressure they and the students were experiencing was out of proportion?

2. In what ways did, or did not, Paris use appropriate teacher leadership skills in implementing and providing stewardship of the campus vision?

3. In what ways could Paris enhance her teacher leadership skills to improve the math department climate while also implementing and providing stewardship for the campus vision?

4. Develop a plan to balance stress and anxiety with academic performance among teachers during particularly demanding times such as preparation for high-stakes tests.

5. What can teacher leaders do on the state and national levels to balance the importance of accountability with the reality of stress, pressure, and anxiety for students and faculty?

6. In what ways could teacher leaders work with districts, universities, professional associations, or others to create a balanced plan for accountability and student knowledge assessment without the use of a single-source test?

CONCLUSIONS

This chapter has been about vision. Without vision we do not have momentum toward anything, either personal or professional. It is as important to have a vision in our personal lives as it is in our schools and classrooms. Reality is where we are today in both cases. Vision is where we want to be. Everything we do as teacher leaders should be focused on this purpose.

The development, articulation, implementation, and stewardship of a vision of student productivity and scholarship within the learning community are essential to maximizing student learning. We must have a vision and a well-planned strategy for achieving it. Therefore, as teacher leaders we must

- Collaboratively develop a campus and classroom vision, with input from diverse stakeholders, on which we can all agree
- Identify specific goals to get to the vision and plan on exactly how to reach those goals
- Articulate that vision to the entire learning community to ensure commitment from all stakeholders
- Work the plan by implementing the vision with the support of the learning community
- Provide stewardship of the vision by nurturing and sustaining it on every level

The rest is up to you. I encourage you to take the time to develop a personal vision and mission for your life. Once that is done, everything else, including your career as a teacher leader, will be improved. The benefits you reap in your personal life will be compounded in your school and classroom success because you have an identified vision and a plan to bring it into reality. What could possibly be wrong with that?

Now, go do it.

IT'S UP TO YOU

1. If you were mentoring a new teacher who had no idea what vision is or what the mission of your school is, how would you explain them?

2. Elaborate on the distinctions between vision and goals and the importance of each.

3. Explain the connection between an identified campus vision and goals by which to attain them.

4. Describe the role and function of teacher leadership in regard to each of the following facets: campus vision; campus and classroom productivity and student learning; leadership in the local, state, and federal political arenas; leadership in the global society.

5. Describe and illustrate the role of followers within the concept of teacher leadership. In terms of vision, if teacher leaders need followers, who leads whom, where, and why?

6. Describe the role of vision in influencing the performance of school and community members toward the achievement of organizational goals.

A teacher leader can enhance systematic school improvement by . . .

- Collaborating with all members of the learning community to develop, articulate, implement, and continuously evaluate a common campus vision of excellence
- Teaching students, parents, and other members of the school community that most goals are reachable with persistence, diligence, and hard work
- Working with others to identify specific goals that will help the campus reach its vision and targeting strategies for goal attainment
- Mobilizing necessary resources to reach identified campus goals
- Implementing innovative ideas inside the campus and the classroom
- Being proactive in reading and analyzing new research and trends in education
- Not being afraid to ask for help when it is needed
- Volunteering to participate or take the lead in campus activities
- Promoting a positive attitude that will encourage students to work hard and take calculated risks
- Attending applicable training sessions on developing a vision and building teams

Core Values and Moral Code

Ethics and Integrity for All Time

"Management is doing things right; leadership is doing the right things."

—Peter F. Drucker

CRITICAL ISSUE: THE PROFESSIONAL EDUCATOR'S CORE VALUES AND MORAL CODE

There can be a big difference between what is legal and what is ethical. If you don't believe that, check news reports about how some political contributions are being used by both major political parties. There are multiple reasons why good people deviate from established behaviors and even more reasons why people make poor choices.

Recently there was a man who exhibited the most outlandish attention-seeking behavior imaginable. He deliberately submitted reports and letters to the editor of a small-town "yellow journalism" newspaper citing supposed improprieties of the local school superintendent and school board. However, he never told the whole story. He chose to tell only the parts that would make his targets look bad. Fortunately, most community members ignored anything printed by this paper in favor of the regular press. But enough read and believed anything in print that it was creating significant community gossip. Enough people wondered whether the superintendent and school board had broken state law or used legal yet unethical behavior that the rumors were causing problems.

When confronted, the complainer admitted that he knew the truth and had intentionally misrepresented it. His rationale was that it was not his job to tell the whole truth. He felt it was the job of the superintendent and the board to engage in public debate with him to prove him wrong. They refused.

This person showed absolutely no remorse. He walked the line carefully between breaking the law and staying just inside it. But who could perceive his intentional actions as ethical and moral, especially because they were designed to harm innocent people?

Yes, there is a distinct difference between legal and ethical behavior. Educators who fulfill the basic requirements of their jobs in meeting the needs of students but do not carry their responsibilities to the highest standard of professionalism are certainly within the bounds of legality. Yet is it ethical for an educator, or anyone else, to do less than his or her all to help someone else? Teacher leaders go the extra mile to be servant leaders for as many people as they can.

PHILOSOPHICAL FRAMEWORK

People often refer to ethics and integrity together as if they were the same thing. They are not. But they do interact. Ethics is a system of moral standards or values. Integrity is a person's honor and sincerity. The two work together in our lives to define who we are and what our character is. Our ethics define who we are as people and, collectively, as a society.

There is no better indicator of ethics than how we treat, interact with, and meet the needs of children. The No Child Left Behind (NCLB) Act was developed in a bipartisan effort to improve student performance. For various reasons, it has never achieved its full potential. However, few could argue with the philosophy and intent on which it was developed.

But NCLB is not enough. Furthermore, no form of legislation ever will be enough. It is up to individuals to take a strong stand for what is good, what is right, and what is of benefit to students of all ages. That means it is up to us.

- Are you ready for this challenge?
- Can you handle this responsibility?
- What does your response to these questions say about your ethics and integrity?
- How can we make schools, classrooms, and learning better?

Ethics: The Established Core Values and Moral Code

Each of us must decide what our core values are. Core values are defined herein as the most important values, the central part of our lives. They are what we stand for and what we are willing to put on the line for the sake of honor and integrity. They are established within us and are the guiding principles of how we live our lives.

In like manner, our moral code consists of the personal standards we set for ourselves in how we exist and act and how we can be predicted to respond to any given issue or event. Our core values are manifested in our personal moral code. Have you ever heard anyone say, "I knew you would say that!" or "I knew that is what he would do!" When someone says those things, they are based on an inner prediction of how someone will think, feel, or act. That inner prediction is how or what others perceive our core values and moral code to be. The problem comes when another's perception of us is not consistent with how we perceive ourselves. If that occurs, it is time to stop, do some serious, in-depth, soulful reflection, and take stock of who we are, why others perceive us as they do, and what we can do to improve the situation.

Integrity: Identifying Your Personal Core Values and Moral Code

Figure 3.1 shows how our personal core values and moral code carry over into every aspect of our lives. You do not have two sets of core values or two different moral codes. You have one set of core values and one moral code that defines who you are as a teacher leader and who you are as a person.

Socrates taught that all truth lies inside the individual and that only by questioning ourselves and our belief systems can we ever find truth (Overholser, 1992). Based on that premise, take your time and slowly answer the following questions. Remember, there are no right or wrong answers, only truthful or nontruthful responses. There is an easy road of quick answers, and there is a longer, tougher road that leads to true introspection and the gaining of new knowledge. The choice is up to you.

- What are your core values, the things that are the most important to you?
- What would other people say are your core values?
- How do your core values guide your actions as both a citizen and a teacher leader?
- In what ways could you enhance your personal and professional behaviors based on the identification of your core values?

Figure 3.1   Reciprocal Determination Cycle

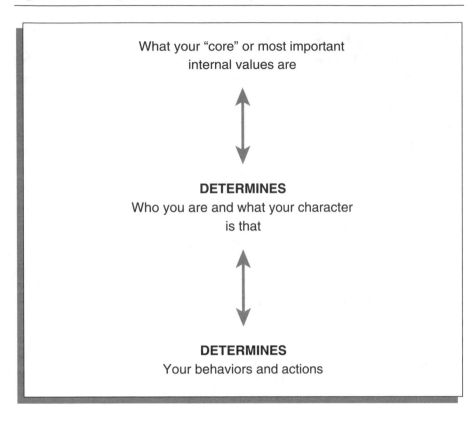

What your "core" or most important
internal values are

DETERMINES
Who you are and what your character
is that

DETERMINES
Your behaviors and actions

Fairness: Extending Your Core Values and Moral Code

A major complaint in schools today is that some people, whether students, parents, or teachers, are sometimes treated differently from others. Most people can accept the consequences of their actions and decisions if they know they are being treated fairly and equitably. Earlier I asked you to take significant time to identify, reflect on, and refine your core values and moral code. Let's carry these answers a little further.

- In what ways can you as a teacher leader use your core values and moral code in decision making in your school and classroom?
- Describe a situation in which a student was treated without consistency, fairness, or equity.
- How would you have handled the situation differently?
- In what ways would your projected behavior have manifested your core values and moral code?

- Describe a situation from your own past in which you wish you had handled a situation differently.
- Explain why you wish you had handled it differently and what you have learned from the experience.

Professional Demeanor: Your Core Values and Moral Code for the Future

Identifying your core values and moral code is the first step toward using them as a teacher leader. Your core values may have been in place all along. However, once you have identified them you will be more conscious of how to use them in your daily behavior and leadership style. Very seldom does a teacher leader identify core values that are surprising. Most teacher leaders include basic moral concepts such as honesty and a focus on students. These are basic values most could agree on.

- How are you manifesting your core values and moral code in your daily life as a citizen? As a teacher leader?
- What kinds of things could you change in your life and career, based on the identification of your core values and moral code?
- How can you use these discoveries to help improve society, with long-standing results?

PROBLEM-BASED LEARNING

Ethics: Does This Guy Have Ethical or Mental Problems?

Teachers at Rick Gregory Elementary School were frustrated and discouraged. They viewed their principal, Rock Hassleback, as both unprofessional and unethical. He played favorites, but whoever his favorite was one day might or might not be his favorite the next day. He bestowed favors on those he liked and overtly distorted the truth about those he did not. Outwardly arrogant and egotistical yet internally insecure, Hassleback was threatened by teachers he viewed as strong or successful. Instead of supporting and applauding their efforts and results, he aimed his most vicious attacks at them. Anyone who attempted to talk to him about his behaviors became his next enemy. He would tell lies about them to his superiors to undermine their credibility, belittle them to their peers, treat them rudely in public, and seek to embarrass them in meetings.

The teachers at Rick Gregory finally got fed up. They selected two of their best teacher leaders, Paula and Regina, to represent them and go talk to the district personnel director, Ms. Davis, about Hassleback's behavior, his apparent lack of a moral compass, or the possibility of a health or mental problem. They gave specific, concrete examples and focused on situations of which Ms. Davis had at least some knowledge. They also urged her to check the teacher retention rate at their campus against others in the district. High-quality teachers were either leaving the district completely or requesting transfers to other campuses at a higher rate than peer schools, they asserted. The worst part, they claimed, was that Mr. Hassleback knew exactly what he was doing and went so far as to lay plans ahead of time on how he would hurt teachers who were his current targets. The campus culture and climate were far less than ideal for implementing the school vision.

Ms. Davis listened attentively to their concerns but also said she had never witnessed Hassleback as being anything but gracious and professional. "That's the way he treats you," Paula and Regina said. "But it is certainly not the way he treats us." Ms. Davis promised to give the situation due consideration and take any appropriate actions. Before leaving, both Paula and Regina expressed their deep concern that if Ms. Davis let Mr. Hassleback know who had come to see her, he would make their work environment very, very bad. Ms. Davis promised that she would not disclose their identities.

Unfortunately, Ms. Davis was not reliable. Shortly after Paula and Regina left her office, she was on the phone with Mr. Hassleback, expressing her concern over the campus climate and culture. It did not take many strategically placed questions from Mr. Hassleback before he had determined where Ms. Davis's concern came from. Because teacher unions were illegal in their state, the teachers felt they had nowhere else to turn. Consequently, they became more and more distraught, and the campus culture and climate suffered.

Think About It

1. How do you think campus teachers, including Paula and Regina, demonstrated leadership skills?

2. In what ways could Paula, Regina, and the rest of the teachers enhance their own professionalism to enhance ethical school leadership?

3. Should Paula and Regina have gone to discuss their principal with Ms. Davis? Why or why not?

4. Was the behavior of the following individuals ethical or unethical? Support your answers.

   Mr. Hassleback

   Paula and Regina

   Ms. Davis

5. What else could the campus have done to address and improve Mr. Hassleback's behavior?

6. As a teacher leader, what would you do if your campus was in this situation? Explain why you would take these actions.

Integrity: Put Me In, Coach!

As head coach of the middle school football team, Coach Kaade Todd thought he had seen and heard everything. But that was before he encountered Malcolm Mellis, father of student athlete Jeremy Mellis. Jeremy, a seventh grader, had potential to be the starting quarterback for the middle school team the next year. He was also a good student and was liked by teachers and fellow students.

Unfortunately, his father was a complete pain in the neck. A genuine coach wanna-be, Malcolm felt it was his responsibility to attend every practice, to yell at the boys and the coaches, and then to follow Kaade to the gym after practice to tell him everything he had done wrong. He did this in detail and with illustrations.

Kaade could have handled that. After all, he had dealt with overzealous fathers many times in his 15 years of teaching and coaching. But Malcolm was different. His "input" did not stop at the gym doors. He felt it was his civic responsibility to spread his "input" to anyone who would listen, even if he or she didn't want to. He did this to the principal, the superintendent, multiple school board members, and, worst of all, local newspaper reporters, who felt it was their civic responsibility to print every word of it.

Needless to say, what Malcolm told people was the truth with a twist. He told only the parts of the story he wanted to tell and intentionally left out the rest, which explained what was really taking place.

Although Kaade's friends and the principal understood what was taking place and supported him, his superintendent was beginning to receive pressure from some school board members to either get Malcolm to shut up or get Kaade out of there. They were tired of having to defend the situation in the community.

In response, Kaade scheduled one more meeting with Malcolm. His goal was to persuade Malcolm to stop generating half-truths and spreading them in the community. Unfortunately, Malcolm had come to enjoy the attention he was getting over being an "athletic activist." He said that if Kaade prevented him from attending practices, he would tell everyone that he was being discriminated against and that Kaade was taking it out on his son. Furthermore, he threatened to claim that his civil liberties were being denied him.

Think About It

1. How did Kaade demonstrate leadership skills in dealing with Malcolm?

2. In what ways could Kaade enhance his teacher leadership skills in dealing with out-of-control parents?

3. Malcolm had problems understanding or applying integrity in his life. In what ways can teachers work with parents and students to instill in them the importance of integrity in a free and democratic society and within the school?

4. The press also displayed a lack of integrity by printing stories without checking the facts. Their primary interest was selling papers, and Malcolm was stirring up enough controversy to help them do that. Was there anything Kaade could do to reason with the press, or was this strictly an administrative issue? Support your response.

5. Kaade has successfully taught and coached for 15 years. After going through a nightmare such as this, should he use his previous successes as a teacher leader in the classroom and request to be released from his coaching position? Or should he stick it out and continue both teaching and coaching? Support your response from an ethical and moral position.

6. Sooner or later almost all teachers have contact with parents or community members who do not display ethical and moral conduct. Integrity does not seem to be important in their lives. What are some proactive things teacher leaders can do to prevent out-of-control behaviors from internal or external stakeholders?

Fairness: Walking the Line

Aubrey was a 10-year-old autistic student enrolled in fourth grade. His Admission, Review, or Dismissal (ARD) committee had placed him in a regular fourth-grade classroom with support from special services on a trial basis to maximize efforts to use the least restrictive environment. The committee had suggested Alison Bailey as his teacher because she was known as both a teacher leader and a compassionate instructor who had successfully dealt with students with various handicaps in the past.

Alison responded positively to having Aubrey in her class and worked hard to individualize and make allowances for his special circumstances. Still, on occasion Aubrey experienced disruptive outbursts. Alison, Aubrey's parents, the campus principal, and the school support staff had a close, cohesive relationship and tried to address each outburst in a developmentally appropriate manner. All in all, they thought the placement was going as well as possible.

Unfortunately, some parents of other students were not so understanding. They resented the outbursts to which their children were subjected and thought Aubrey should be moved to a self-contained classroom. In a patient manner, Alison tried to explain Aubrey's special needs and learning differences to them. Some became more patient. Others did not.

In hindsight, Alison wished she had held a parent meeting to explain Aubrey's situation, his special needs, and how they could work together to make his life better. In discussing this with her principal, she was told there were legal issues regarding privacy that had prevented this from happening. Alison's struggle with the legal issues caused her internal turmoil as she also struggled with ethical concerns for every student in the classroom. Was it fair to Aubrey to disclose private information to the parents of other students in her classroom? On the other hand, was it fair to the rest of the students and their parents to not let them know what was happening in the classroom?

Think About It

1. How did Alison demonstrate teacher leadership skills with students, administrators, and parents?

2. In what ways could Alison further enhance her teacher leadership skills to help meet the needs of handicapped students?

3. Is it appropriate to place a child with special needs in a regular classroom? What ethical, moral, and fairness issues are involved?

4. What legal issues must teacher leaders be aware of and in compliance with in regard to the privacy rights of handicapped students? Give examples of how they should be applied.

(Continued)

(Continued)

> 5. After Aubrey began having outbursts in the classroom, which the rest of the class observed, what could Alison have done out of fairness to everyone while maintaining her ethical, confidential, and legal responsibilities?
>
> 6. Does your state have a teacher Code of Conduct? If so, describe it. If not, what are the most important issues you feel should be addressed in such a code?

Professional Demeanor: Why's Everybody Always Picking on Me?

The kindergarten teachers at the Kathy Lynn Martin Early Childhood Center felt honored because each year selected teachers were able to attend the state Early Childhood conference on school funds. The teachers were on a rotating schedule such that each of them would have a turn within a specified period. The district paid for their substitute teachers, absorbed all costs related to the conference, and counted their absences from school toward professional development. Each year the teachers looked forward to hearing excited reports from the teachers who attended the conference. Because the district used a rotating schedule and paid the costs, every teacher felt empowered and felt that the district supported the enhancement of their teacher leadership skills.

Unfortunately, sometimes a teacher's out-of-town behavior is not as professional as the district expects. This year Cinnamon, a second-year teacher, turned out to be less than committed to the purpose of the trip. Whereas the other teachers got up early each morning to attend and learn from every session available, Cinnamon chose to sleep late the first morning and missed the first two sessions. The reason she was so tired was because she had stayed out late having a very good time. When she finally did show up for sessions, she was grumpy and unable to concentrate.

Cinnamon should have learned from her bad experience the first day, but she did not. After a late afternoon nap, she again stayed out late and didn't make it back to the room she was sharing with another sleeping teacher until the early morning. The next day, she didn't bother to get up at all. When the rest of the teachers finished the conference at noon and returned to the hotel to check out, Cinnamon was still asleep. They had to wake her and rush her to leave so they would not miss the hotel checkout time. Although they were excited about the things they had learned and anxious to share with their colleagues at school, they were not happy with Cinnamon's unprofessional behavior.

Returning to school the next week, Cinnamon was rested and cheerful. She did not understand why the other teachers she had traveled with treated her coolly or why they refused to help her put together her presentation to the faculty on what she had learned at the conference. She thought it was unprofessional of them not to help her. The other teachers thought it was Cinnamon's own fault for not being adequately prepared to make her presentation. If she had not stayed out for two nights and slept for two mornings, she would have attended more sessions, learned new teaching strategies, and had many things to share with the faculty. They thought attending the sessions was the purpose for the trip and the reason the school had invested time and resources in letting them go.

Think About It

1. In what ways could Cinnamon enhance her teacher leadership skills to improve her credibility and responsibility as a professional educator?

2. Would it have been appropriate for the other teachers on the trip to talk to Cinnamon about her absence from conference sessions and encourage her to be present while they were still there? Or was her behavior none of their business? Explain your answer.

3. Was it unprofessional of the other teachers to not help Cinnamon prepare her faculty presentation? Why or why not?

4. Cinnamon thought the other teachers were making more out of her absences than they should have and asserted that she was every bit as professional as any of them. What do you think, and why?

5. From the perspective of teacher leaders, what could be done to prevent situations like this from happening again in the future?

6. Describe a situation you have experienced in which a teacher did not exhibit professional or personal demeanor. As a teacher leader, what could you do to resolve the situation and make it a learning opportunity for all involved?

CONCLUSIONS

In this chapter we have identified and discussed the importance of ethics and integrity to you as a person and as a teacher leader. We have sought in-depth self-awareness by identifying and explaining the concept of core values and how they relate to your individual moral code. Furthermore, you have looked within yourself to identify your own core values and moral code and determined ways you can use them to affect the students in your classroom for the greater good.

These are very important issues and should be analyzed with their significance in mind. The more effort you put into really thinking about who you are, what you stand for, how others see you, and whether how others see you matches with how you see yourself, the better off you will be both as a person and as a teacher leader.

In the musical *The King and I,* the British teacher has come to Siam to teach the children of the king. All the customs in Siam are very different from what she is used to. Yet as she gets to know the children, she also begins to love them, and they, in turn, begin to love her. At one point she tells them that there is an ancient saying that when you become a teacher, by your students you will be taught.

This is still true today. Look inside yourself to determine who you are and who you want to be. Create your own personal vision and plan how you will get from who you are now to the person you want to become. Listen to those around you. And remember, when you become a teacher, by your students you will be taught.

IT'S UP TO YOU

1. Is a teacher leader the definer of classroom values? If so, in what ways?

2. How do leaders lead with integrity without being swayed by inappropriate internal or external constituencies?

3. Compare and contrast the distinctions between leaders, rulers, power wielders, and despots. How do the issues of ethics and integrity apply to each?

4. Warren Bennis's philosophy of leadership focuses on the individual capability of the leader. He says leadership is a function of knowing yourself, having a vision that is well communicated, building trust among colleagues, and taking effective action to realize your own leadership potential (Bennis, 1989). Respond to this philosophy from an ethical perspective for teacher leaders. How can trust among colleagues be developed?

5. What values are important in evaluating teacher leadership?

6. In what ways, if any, could a leader lose the ability to lead? Identify and explain what factors could be involved.

*A teacher leader can enhance
systematic school improvement by . . .*

- Following what your heart tells you is right
- Realizing that wherever you are, you represent your school
- Treating people in an equitable manner
- Working with multiple entities to develop a model in which diverse groups can give specific feedback on trust issues and possible perceptions that policies and procedures are not being equally applied to all people
- Facilitating collegial discussions regarding breakdowns in trust and communication with administrators and potential perceptions that teachers and other community voices are not heard or respected
- Collaborating closely with other teachers and administrators to identify possible trust problems between them and engaging each in open discussion about how to resolve the situation
- Exhibiting regular, punctual, and positive attendance at work and all related activities
- Treating other people as you would like to be treated
- Being professional, always acting in a way that would make your parents proud of you

Classroom Culture and Climate

It Can Make You or Break You

"*Leadership is the art of getting someone else to do something you want done.*"

—Dwight D. Eisenhower

CRITICAL ISSUE: CLASSROOM CULTURE AND CLIMATE

Classroom culture and climate often are considered the "soft stuff" that is more important on the elementary level than on the secondary level. But developmentally appropriate classroom culture and climate are necessary to optimum teacher leadership in classrooms and campuses on all levels.

Often the terms *organizational culture* and *organizational climate* are considered ambiguous, confusing, or interchangeable. Yet each has its own distinct meanings and uses. Organizational culture is the way things are done, what things are valued, and how they are put into practice within a unit. Organizational climate is the feel or ethos of the classroom. Let me share a story that will help you see how they are different and why both are important components of teacher leadership (Wilmore, 2004).

A few years ago my husband and I were preparing for a trip with friends. Before the trip I was killing time in a mall before meeting our son for lunch. As I wandered into a store I noticed a table with a large sign that said "Sale." I can't resist a sale, so I went to see what they had.

In browsing I found a cute little wallet with a shoulder strap that would be handy for our trip. In looking at it I could not find a price, so I checked all of the other cute little wallets. There were no price tags or stickers, nor were there any price markings on any of them.

Carrying one of the wallets with me, I went to the cash register and asked the employee, "Can you tell me how much this is?" I didn't think that was such an odd request, but apparently it was. The lady looked at me as if I were stupid, took the wallet, and looked it over. When she didn't find a price tag either, she opened it. There was no price tag inside. At this point the employee looked at me as if it was my fault. She heaved a heavy "Hummm" and walked to the table, which was still clearly labeled "Sale."

At the table she did exactly what I had done and checked all of them. No pricing. Now she was really irritated and looked at me as if I had removed the price tags myself. If I hadn't been really interested in the wallet, I would have left. The lady now walked back to the cash register, scanned the bar code, and told me a price.

Then I really ticked her off by saying, "Is that the regular price or the sale price?" Again, she looked at me as if I was beyond the stupidest person she had ever met and said, "It's not on sale." By now, I was the one feeling exasperated, but I maintained my manners as I pointed to the table with the large sign that clearly said "Sale." The employee looked at her register again, then at me, and said, "They are not on sale."

At this point, I very sweetly said, "Thank you," and walked out. Enough was enough.

Still killing time, I wandered into another store, where an employee promptly greeted me and asked whether she could help me. I declined but continued into the store, noticing immediately the difference in the feel, the climate, of the two stores. During my brief stay in the second store, several other employees also smiled and greeted me, asking if they could assist me in any way. Shortly thereafter I left but not without making several purchases for the trip, none of which I can remember today. Yet I still remember how I was treated over that cute little wallet.

The point of this story is that the two stores are classic examples of organizations with vastly different cultures and climates. One was cold, not helpful, and ultimately unproductive because I didn't buy anything. The second was warm, welcoming, and solicitous. Their organizational cultures and climates were opposites. So were their results and productivity. I bought nothing at one store and several items at the other. Which organizational culture and climate were the most effective? Draw your own conclusions.

The same is true in schools. Even a stranger can tell the difference in how some classrooms feel. This is their classroom climate. The way a campus and classroom feel is a top priority for parents as they contemplate, and hope for, their children's classroom assignments. One thing parents find supremely important is the learning environment their children will be part of. Most parents want their children to be nurtured and cared for as individuals. I have yet to meet a parent who asks for his or her child to be placed in a classroom with a cold climate (Beaudoin & Taylor, 2004).

The two stores described here also had different cultures. Obviously, steps to provide for the needs of customers were addressed in vastly different ways in each setting. They addressed their marketing techniques in opposite manners. They also got opposite results in reaching their goal: making sales.

The same is true in regard to classroom culture. There is more to classroom culture than the ethnicity of its occupants. The culture of the classroom is identified by the things that are valued therein. These are easily identified by the effects achieved rather than the ideals espoused. Ultimately, the classroom climate and culture are strong determinants of success in the goal of maximizing student learning.

PHILOSOPHICAL FRAMEWORK

An Ethos of Learning Expectations, Appreciation, and Success

There are several important components to a highly successful classroom culture and climate. As shown in Figure 4.1, all are necessary to optimize student success. Schools that experience the greatest success have an ethos, or atmosphere, of high learning expectations for all students, appreciation for both students and faculty, and a high probability of success for everyone. They expect their students to do well, and, not surprisingly, their students learn and do well. These schools are also filled with many teacher leaders who have high expectations for their students and themselves.

This ethos transposes itself into a campus culture and climate that promote and expect success. Teacher leaders thrive in this environment and replicate it in their own classrooms. They appreciate the efforts of every student and parent and let them know it in a genuine manner. Not surprisingly, success tends to breed success. One of the biggest obstacles for students who have previously struggled academically is that they do not see themselves succeeding. Their inner perception is that they cannot be successful; therefore, they see themselves continuing to struggle. Too often this results in these same students dropping out of school as soon as they can. They have no expectation of academic success; therefore, they do not achieve it. Many of them also have discipline problems because they perceive negative reinforcement as better than no reinforcement at all. Therefore, they act up, create havoc, and make nuisances of themselves just to get any attention at all.

Figure 4.1   Successful Students Need High-Quality Classroom Culture and Climate

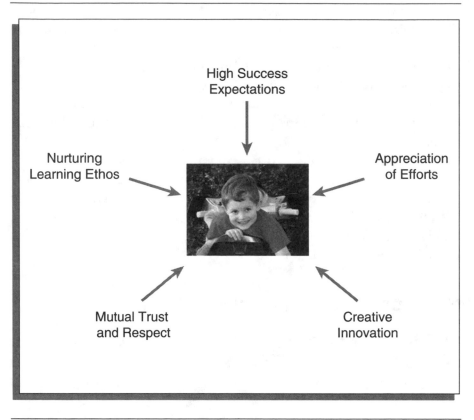

Source: Photo reprinted with permission from Wes Rollen.

Teacher leaders do their best to not let themselves become involved in anything negative, and they do not want their students to be part of anything that could adversely affect the school or classroom culture or climate. Rather than letting a student become discouraged when struggling academically or personally, a teacher leader will work with him or her individually. A teacher leader will diversify instructional strategies and make all efforts necessary to encourage students to believe they can be successful. All of these actions are typical of teacher leaders who seek to nurture and sustain a culture and climate that values student success in all its varied forms.

Another important thing about teacher leaders is that they are not afraid to ask for help, if necessary, in meeting the needs of a specific student. It may sound paradoxical to call someone a teacher leader, then say he or she is asking for help. But true leaders in any venue are never afraid to ask for help when needed. They have confidence in their own abilities, but they know that there is strength in asking for direction when direction is needed. This calm confidence in their ability to ask for help may be the tool that changes a student's life. Asking for help is not a bad thing. It is a very, very good thing for all concerned.

Another very important strategy teacher leaders use to promote a nurturing classroom culture and climate is to make sure their students realize that they are trying hard and that their efforts are truly appreciated. There is nothing as detrimental to organizational productivity as to expect someone of any age to work unbelievably hard, then act as if his or her efforts and hard work have been no big deal. No one likes to feel unappreciated. Furthermore, no one should be made to feel ordinary. No one likes to feel ordinary. Everyone likes to feel appreciated, loved, and cared about. Everyone likes to feel that their ideas are important and noteworthy. In short, no one likes to be ignored or taken advantage of.

Take care of your people. Treasure them whether they are 6 or 60 years old. Let them know you care, and be sure that you really do. Caring is the basis on which teacher leadership is founded. It is emotionally exhausting and can drain you completely. But truly caring is the underpinning on which teacher leaders build their classrooms. Care about your students. Work with them to let them know and believe that they will be successful. Remember, actions speak far louder than words. In fact, words without action mean nothing. Appreciate students' hard work, then sit back and watch their attitudes and work ethics improve (Hoyle, 2001; Pellicer, 2003).

Change in attitude and perceptions may not occur overnight. As our beloved physician, Dr. O. T. Smyth, once told when I was quite run down, "Elaine, you didn't get in this shape overnight, and you won't get out of it overnight." He was right. The point is that change often does not happen immediately (Ackerman & Mackenzie, 2006). As teacher leaders we must be patient and build a firm foundation toward the realization of our classroom and campus vision. The classroom is where real change starts and from which success flows. Classroom improvement affects the entire school. It is worth the wait.

Mutual Trust and Respect

In order for the desired success-generating change to occur, there must be mutual trust and respect among all members of the learning community. Teachers and administrators must respect parents, and parents must respect them also. Only a generation ago parents generally always supported the school. Regrettably, things have turned in the wrong direction. Too often parents are confrontational and take exception to anything that doesn't go the way they want it to, regardless if it is right, wrong, or in the best interest of their child. This is a sad thing and is not based on mutual trust and respect. It is also not healthy for our society at large because it indicates a lack of trust and respect toward the established educational society. As responsive teacher leaders we are taking steps to improve this.

Likewise, teachers and administrators must also engage in active listening to develop, maintain, and enhance their relationships and the learning environment. Optimized student productivity cannot occur without trust, respect, and fairness. The same is true in classrooms between teachers and students. Sincerity, trust, respect, and appreciation on all levels will beget sincerity, trust, respect, and appreciation, which will ultimately improve student performance. Teacher leaders thrive on improved student performance and will do whatever they can to ensure that it occurs.

Innovation

We cannot keep leading instruction in the same old ways and expect to get different results. Society and demographics are changing at a rapid pace. As long as we keep on doing what we have always done, we will keep on getting what we have always gotten. This is not good enough. Classrooms with straight little chairs where everyone looks and acts exactly alike are not coming back. Teacher leaders realize that global society is in the midst of great cultural change. It is up to us to lead the challenge of meeting the needs of all students regardless of their race, culture, faith, or economic background. Education is the key not only to their future but also to the future of our country. It will be the legacy of our generation. All great societies are judged by the value they place on education. America today is no different. It is time to leave our comfort zones and to take great risks through different instructional strategies to meet the needs of every student in our schools (Fullan, 2001).

Being a risk taker does not mean blindly throwing together lesson plans that are not research based or composed of best practices. Teacher leaders know that creating change in classrooms takes a great deal of time. It takes great effort to research, implement, and evaluate the best ways to help each individual student succeed.

It may sound as if I am implying that teacher leaders should have an Individualized Education Plan (IEP) for every child. In an ideal world every student would have a trained professional working and planning lessons on his or her exact level, for each subject, to interest and engage the student and to modify as necessary to guarantee his or her success. That would be incredibly expensive and is not likely to happen. That leaves us to fill the gap. In an ideal world, every student would receive innovative, individualized attention. Wouldn't that be wonderful? Until money and resources for schools start growing on trees, teacher leaders must be innovative thinkers who do whatever is necessary to get appropriate resources to meet the learning needs of children. They think innovatively and are proud of it. They are risk takers who see a problem, analyze it, and ask themselves, "What can I do about this? How can I make it better?" Then they do it. They don't wait for someone else to take the lead. They solicit collaboration in the learning community and then do what they can every single day to meet the needs of each student who enters the classroom (Glaser, 2004; Rubin, 2002). That is being a teacher leader.

PROBLEM-BASED LEARNING

An Ethos of Learning Expectations, Appreciation, and Success: What Was I Thinking When I Said I Would . . . ?

Teachers in the Ingleside public schools were asked to volunteer time and energy in the development of a large grant that would greatly enhance the technology of the district. The work would involve investigating everything from hardware and software to student-used laptop computers in classrooms. Teachers were needed for input on everything from financial considerations to substantiating the need for the advanced technology and what impact it would have on student learning for Pre–K students through high school. In short, it was a very large project and would take a great deal of time, research, and effort.

To few people's surprise, not as many teachers volunteered as had been hoped for. Although some district leaders were experts in their fields who could assist and guide them, the small group of teacher leaders ended up with much more work than they had anticipated. They had to do this in addition to their regular teaching responsibilities and extracurricular work because the district could not afford to pay substitutes or give them release time. Worse, the district had not heard about the grant until late in the game, so the teacher leaders had to work on a very short timeline. By the end, they were proud of their work but very, very tired physically, mentally, and emotionally. In fact, most of them were saying that if anyone ever asked them to volunteer for anything that had to do with grant procurement in the future, they were going to run in the other direction. Although they were not complaining, the teachers did not feel appreciated. They were just plain worn out.

The grant prospectus was finalized in the district central administration office. Recognizing the incredibly low morale among the volunteers, the district honored each one with a comp day each, to be taken in lieu of a traditional inservice work day, recognition in front of the school board at their regular monthly meeting, and certificates of appreciation, which were distributed at the school board meeting with copies placed in the teachers' personnel records. This was done before results of the grant prospectus were known, thus helping the teachers to feel their work was appreciated regardless of the consequences of the prospectus. Once the worn-out teachers had the chance to get some sleep and these appreciative efforts were made, they felt a strong sense of personal achievement.

Think About It

1. How did these teachers demonstrate leadership skills?

2. Brainstorm additional strategies the district could have used to complete the grant prospectus on time without putting so much stress on the limited number of volunteers.

3. Was it appropriate to ask teachers to develop the grant prospectus when they already had full-time teaching jobs and some thought that the central office staff should be doing this? Explain your answer.

4. Was it appropriate to give these teachers a day of comp time when other teachers also volunteer their time for other projects outside the regular school day? Why or why not?

5. In what additional ways could the district have shown appreciation to the teachers?

6. If the grant is not funded, will this take away from the sense of empowerment the teachers felt upon completion of the difficult task? Why or why not?

Mutual Trust and Respect: Twinkle, Twinkle, Little Star, What You Say Is What You Are

Jandi was a third-year elementary teacher who had recently relocated with her husband. She was hired to teach fourth grade in an elementary school with an experienced staff. Although this would be Jandi's first year of teaching fourth grade, she had taught on other levels. She was excited about teaching in a new arena and looking forward to the new experience.

There were three other fourth-grade teachers at the school. In the beginning, all of them were very friendly and helpful. But as the year progressed it came to Jandi's attention that one of them, Margaret, was talking about her and making fun of her behind her back. This hurt her feelings and undermined her confidence in her teaching abilities in her new grade assignment and campus.

At first Jandi ignored what she had learned and hoped it was incorrect. But as time went by she learned that not only was it true, but it was getting worse. In fact, there were times when she would walk into the teacher workroom and all talking would cease. In each of these instances, Margaret was present.

Jandi did not know what to do. The situation was tearing her up inside. She did not want to speak to the principal about it for fear he would think she was a crybaby or not up to the task of dealing with the other teachers. Worse, she was somewhat afraid he would think the things Margaret was saying were true.

Finally, she went to the most senior of the fourth-grade teachers, Mrs. Satterwhite, and poured her heart out. Mrs. Satterwhite was very kind to her and told her to ignore Margaret. She said Margaret was just jealous of the success Jandi was having by using instructional techniques that Margaret herself was not comfortable with. Furthermore, Mrs. Satterwhite told Jandi that this was not new behavior from Margaret and that everyone knew how she was. "Just ignore it and go on," she said. "You are doing just fine."

Jandi felt much better after talking to Mrs. Satterwhite, but the idea that anyone was talking about her behind her back still bothered her a great deal. She felt she could no longer respect or trust Margaret. After talking with Mrs. Satterwhite she also knew other people's respect and trust of her would depend on how she handled the situation with Margaret. The whole thing frustrated her.

Think About It

1. As a teacher still early in her career, how did Jandi demonstrate maturity in this awkward situation?

2. In what additional ways could Jandi have enhanced her teacher leadership skills?

3. Did Jandi handle the situation in an appropriately professional manner? Why or why not?

(Continued)

(Continued)

4. What additional things could Jandi have done to improve the situation with Margaret? Should she confront Margaret? Why or why not?

5. Margaret's words were not falling on deaf ears; others were listening. Mrs. Satterwhite acknowledged what was going on, and Jandi herself had walked in on conversations of which she felt she was the subject. What should the other teachers have done in regard to both Margaret and Jandi to ensure a campus culture and climate of mutual respect and trust for all?

6. What could Jandi learn from this situation, and how should she handle it if anything like this ever happens again?

Innovation: If We Build It, They Will Come

The Patriot School District was in the early stages of discussing the development and implementation of an alternative middle and high school campus for students with atypical learning styles. They were focused on developing not a dumping ground for district discipline problems but a truly innovative school for students who learned in ways that were not conducive to a traditional campus structure and framework. One of the first things they did was send a call to any district teachers who would be interested in serving on a committee to research, discuss, analyze, and make a recommendation to the district as to the potential of such a campus.

Because the committee was made up of volunteer teachers who had an interest in the subject, the group bonded early and well. They had lively discussions, conducted research on alternative school frameworks and learning styles, divided up tasks, made visits to various schools in other locations, discussed various options, got input from others inside and outside the locality, sought consensus, and made a strong recommendation to their district administration for a campus that would be a composite of all the best practices they had studied or seen. This campus would be totally different not only from their current middle and high schools but also from any known alternative schools that catered to the learning styles of students. They were proud that they had been empowered to explore and come up with their own plan and proud that their district trusted them to be both creative and thorough. Once they made their recommendations, they waited to see what action, if any, the district would take.

Think About It

1. How did the teachers involved in studying this project demonstrate leadership skills?

2. In what ways did the teachers involved with the project enhance their own professionalism and knowledge by volunteering their time, energy, and commitment to this endeavor?

3. What logic and motivational theory, if any, did the district follow to empower teacher leaders to investigate and develop such an important proposal?

4. Was it a good or bad idea to let teacher leaders become so empowered with an idea that the district might decide not to use? What precautions should or could be taken? Support your response.

5. Should the teacher leaders who were so actively involved and supportive be given the first chance to teach in the new school if it is implemented? Why or why not? What impact, if any, could this have on remaining teachers?

6. If the idea is not adopted, what can be done to prevent these hardworking teacher leaders from becoming disengaged and disconnected from future research projects?

CONCLUSIONS

In order for schools, classrooms, and students to be successful, teacher leaders must generate a culture and climate that are focused on the needs of students and based on mutual trust and respect throughout the learning community. Teacher leaders must be willing to do unusual things to meet the varying needs of their students. This includes addressing more facets of the student's life than just academics. Teacher leaders must have a zeal for helping students succeed and using creative problem solving.

The culture and climate of every school and classroom are different. Teacher leaders work hard to ensure that their classrooms are truly centered on the needs of the students by paying close attention to various nuances in their lives. They realize that teaching is far more than conveying knowledge. Teacher leaders are not afraid to let their students know that they care about them. Teacher leaders know that everyone in the learning community must work together to promote student success and the campus vision of excellence in an atmosphere of mutual trust and respect. Finally, teacher leaders constantly look for ways to do everything better, to be more innovative, and to be more creative, always with a focus on maximizing student success. Can we count on you?

IT'S UP TO YOU

1. Compare and contrast the importance of both organizational culture and climate in a school and classroom setting.

2. Describe the distinctions between and significance of campus and classroom culture and climate.

3. What are the distinctions in leadership roles between a teacher leader and a campus administrator in creating an effective campus culture and climate? Where do they overlap, and where are they different?

4. How does a leader's personality affect her or his effectiveness, if at all? Explain your answer.

5. What is the role of the leader's personality in facilitating a nurturing classroom culture and climate?

6. How do the culture and climate of a classroom affect organizational productivity through increased student learning?

A teacher leader can enhance systematic school improvement by . . .

- Collaborating in campus team-building exercises to identify the desired campus culture and climate and specific ways this culture and climate can be implemented and improved
- With other campus stakeholders, jointly hosting newcomer sessions to assist new faculty and staff in acclimating to the campus culture and climate
- Acting as a servant leader at all times
- Developing and encouraging systematic communication mechanisms to help manage change within the organizational culture and climate
- Treating all people with respect and dignity regardless of the situation or how they are acting
- Remaining unbiased in all situations and in decision making
- Encouraging greater faculty and student participation in all campus and team-building activities
- Jointly cultivating and maintaining with administrators a positive atmosphere even when difficult situations arise

- Providing a classroom and campus environment that facilitates active student learning
- Leading brainstorming sessions to address teacher concerns and facilitate the implementation of needed changes
- Following up with faculty, staff, and administrators after changes are implemented to see whether the concerns are being adequately addressed
- Promoting a safe, orderly campus environment and caring for all people at all times

Curriculum and Instruction for Today's Classrooms

Not for the Faint of Heart

"Don't tell people how to do things. Tell them what to do and let them surprise you with their results."

—General George S. Patton

CRITICAL ISSUE: CURRICULUM AND INSTRUCTION

Curriculum is what we teach. Instruction is how we teach it. There are as many instructional strategies as there are students to teach. Finding the most developmentally appropriate techniques to maximize instruction for every student is not easy. In fact, many would consider it far too time consuming, challenging, and emotionally draining to be possible. Teacher leaders seek to do everything realistically possible to generate student success. Student success is teacher success. No teacher is ultimately successful if his or her students are not. Teachers may have the fanciest lesson plans imaginable, but if their students are not learning, they are not successful.

The only real way to do this is to study multiple forms of student assessment data, determine student strengths and weaknesses, identify pupils' best learning styles, and plan appropriate instruction for each student based on those needs. If you think that is idealistic, I readily admit that it is. Being the change agent within a campus often is not easy. Bringing high expectations and individualizing student needs is a critical part of becoming a teacher leader. After all, change has to begin with someone. It may as well be us. Set a high standard of teaching and learning in your classroom. Let the success of your students motivate other teachers to follow your model of meeting student needs, no matter how time consuming and challenging they are.

In September 2005, Hurricane Rita slammed into the Texas Gulf Coast and hit our hometown, Port Arthur, Texas. Because we now live in the Dallas area our extended family came to our house for safety. They stayed with us for almost a month. It wasn't that they did not want to go home. They were not allowed to return because of the lack of clean water and electricity. We enjoyed having them with us for an extended period of time.

It was interesting to see how the educational needs of our four evacuated school-aged nieces and nephews were addressed. The high school twins enrolled in our local school district. However, their family had decided before the beginning of the school year to homeschool the two younger girls. Therefore, during their time with us their schooling continued in our kitchen. My youngest niece did well, but my older one foundered, which caused disharmony in an already tense situation. When I got home from the university one day I was told, "Sarah fell asleep on her math." Notice that she fell asleep *on* her math papers, not *during* her math lesson.

That child was *bored.*

Shouldn't that tell us something? When any student falls asleep during instruction, something is wrong. It does not matter whether the student is being homeschooled or attends a public or private school. Students who are actively engaged in learning do not fall asleep during instruction.

One of our twins had done the same thing in the past, and his teachers did not appreciate Sam's classroom slumber. In both instances there is a common thread: Both students were bored. No student should be bored with learning. If a student is bored, something is wrong. Of course, it is not good for a student to sleep in class. However, if any student is sleeping in class, the *cause* of the slumber must be addressed. Is there a problem in the student's personal, family, physical, or emotional life that causes her or him to sleep during class? Or are changes in instruction needed to interest students, keep them awake, and get them actively engaged in learning? In Sam's case a self-paced program in which he could receive credit the moment he completed all course requirements and passed each form of assessment was very successful. Sam is very intelligent. Regular classroom settings bored him. He needed and responded well to challenge. In a self-paced program, he controlled his own destiny. He responded well to the immediate reinforcement of completing his work rapidly. On top of that, his grades improved because he was invested in the process. Suddenly he had a reason to get engaged because the sooner he did what he needed to do, the sooner he was finished. He now had a strong motivation to complete his work in a timely manner: graduation. Sam graduated 3 months early.

Curriculum and instruction are the two basic things that separate schools and classrooms from other organizations such as the retail stores discussed in Chapter 4. Curriculum and instruction are the meat and potatoes of what we do. What can we do as teacher leaders to improve teaching and learning in our classrooms? What impact can these methods have in classrooms beyond our own?

PHILOSOPHICAL FRAMEWORK

Whether we are trying to address the mandates of the No Child Left Behind (NCLB) Act or other standards-based competencies in the state or local arenas, the alignment of curriculum with assessment is a hot topic in America today. Although few dispute the importance of accurate measurement of student learning, the problem often arises from the stress and anxiety this places on students, faculty, administrators, and parents. At what point does the stress become counterproductive? Are the anecdotes of high-stakes testing, stress-related illnesses for students and faculty, and the early retirements of excellent educators exaggerated? Until a longitudinal study can be done, we cannot be sure.

What we do know is that regardless of high-stakes testing, it is the role and responsibility of teacher leaders and everyone else in the learning community to maximize student learning through whatever means necessary. Don't do it for the test. Do it for the kid. That's what learning is all about. As shown in Figure 5.1, many things contribute to improving student performance. One of the most important is an engaging and relevant curriculum.

Engaging and Relevant Curriculum

The first thing that must be done to generate high-level student learning is to make sure students are actively engaged and interested in what they are supposed to be learning. Even as adults, we tend to tune out anything that is not of interest to us. The reason is that whatever is not interesting us is simply not relevant to our daily existence. For example, if I had to sit in long training sessions on auto mechanics, I would be bored out of my mind. Do I think auto mechanics is important? Of course. Is it relevant in my life? Not really. Although I know

Figure 5.1   Factors to Enhance Student Performance

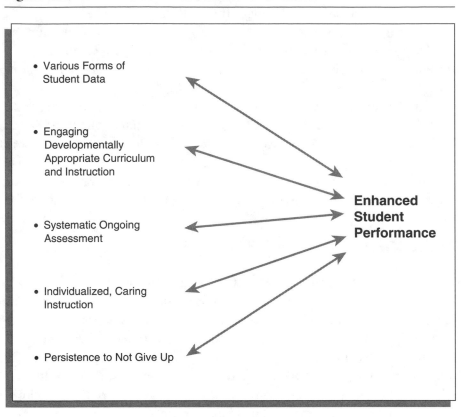

that I should know something about it, I'm not really motivated. Therefore, the whole issue of auto mechanics, however important, has no direct relevance to me. Even as an adult I'm supposed to be able to sit still and pay attention even when I'm bored. I'm not supposed to fall asleep *on* my auto mechanics. The same is true for the PreK–12 learners. They need to be interested, actively engaged, and motivated to maximize their learning opportunities.

The role of teacher leaders is to take responsibility for finding ways to make topics at least somewhat interesting and relevant to students. Furthermore, it is also our role to encourage other teachers to do likewise. This can be done by conducting team meetings and conferences, watching others teach, researching new instructional strategies, brainstorming diverse ways to actively engage students, and brainstorming ways to make learning relevant to students' daily lives. This is easier with some topics than others. As Mary Poppins sings, "A spoonful of sugar helps the medicine go down." Interesting and engaging lessons can be the sugar that helps the learning go down.

Developmentally Appropriate Instructional Strategies

Teacher leaders know the difference between a great lesson plan that looks good on paper and a great lesson plan that is also developmentally appropriate for the students for which it has been created. This comes from the study of child and human development, experience, wisdom, and openness to students' verbal and nonverbal reactions to what is going on around them. If learners are tuned out, something is wrong. It is our job to edit instructional strategies rather than the student's job to change his or her developmental level or learning style. Although this takes more time and effort from us, the results will manifest themselves in increased student learning.

This can be quite a task in heterogeneously grouped classrooms. Yet research shows that students learn best when exposed to real-world scenarios and with other learners who are both like and not like them. Diversity on various levels is one reason many colleges admit some applicants from varying races and backgrounds whose test scores are below the average of the entering class. These colleges realize that all students tend to benefit from a diverse class environment.

Although it is difficult to address instruction from a heterogeneous perspective, it is not impossible. Cooperative learning, peer tutoring, and other strategies have demonstrated long-term effectiveness in mixed-ability groups. Implement peer tutoring, introduce hands-on, kinesthetic activities, and use classroom volunteers. Teacher leaders know that no single instructional technique works for every student every time. They regularly share, conference, and mentor with others to find which teaching techniques match the developmental, academic, emotional, and learning styles of each student. Teacher leaders also realize that what works today for a specific student may not work tomorrow. That is why teacher leaders are flexible, adaptable, and competent enough to change what is not working to something that will work. Instead of Superman, who flies over tall buildings, we have Superteachers, who can change at a moment's notice to address the needs of students. Not everyone can fly or leap over tall buildings or teach students with eclectic learning styles. Only Superteachers can be teacher leaders. It is definitely not for the faint of heart. Are we ready for this challenge? The children of the world need us.

For students to maximize their learning opportunities, teacher leaders and others must work together to ensure that the curriculum being taught is what is being assessed and vice versa (Figure 5.2). Teacher leaders are constantly looking for ways to confirm that they are teaching what they think they are teaching. This is one excellent reason for aligning curriculum with assessment and conducting assessment in a consistent, ongoing manner.

Figure 5.2   Alignment of Curriculum and Assessment

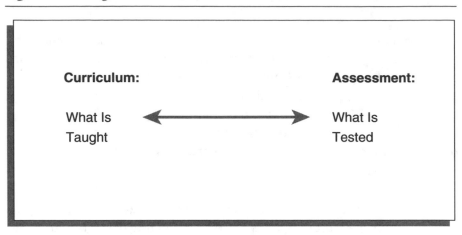

Ongoing Systematic Assessment

To determine whether they need to modify the curriculum or change instructional strategies, teacher leaders use ongoing assessment. For assessment to be ongoing means that it must be continual or taking place all the time. That does not mean a teacher leader is testing all day long. It does mean the teacher is constantly, almost subconsciously, watching and assessing what every student is doing, or capable of doing, at all times and in a systematic manner. The teacher is using various forms of data to enhance individual student performance. In other words, a teacher leader does not just stand, deliver, hope for the best, and give tests at the end of each chapter. A teacher leader is watching all the time. A teacher leader is alert to the academic growth of students. Teacher leaders do this without ceasing. They watch and assess student progress so much that it becomes a part of their natural way of teaching.

The purpose of this constant assessment is to make sure each student is making progress in his or her learning journey. The student may not have arrived at the desired destination, or goal, but at least he or she is making progress. If progress is not occurring, something is wrong. There has to be a reason. Is the student simply not trying? If not, we need to find out why and try to do something about it. If the student needs help in any area, even counseling, the teacher leader works to procure that assistance. If the student is trying and still isn't learning, we find out why not. Does the student have a language problem or a learning disability? Is the student hungry? Does the student have a safe home to return to at the end of the day? Is the student ill? What exactly is going on? A teacher leader researches what is causing the lack of progress and works to eliminate obstacles. It is certainly not the role of the teacher leader to personally solve every problem. It is the role of the teacher leader to facilitate problem solving. In other words, teacher leaders seek to be part of the solution rather than part of the problem. In most cases this can involve working with other educators, families, and often additional resources in the learning community. Teacher leaders never stop working to maximize the learning capability and success of each student every day. Anything less is not to be a teacher leader. A leader must lead. A leader does not give up. A leader always keeps her or his eyes on the goal. In this instance the goal is optimized student learning and progress toward a global democratic society where all people are respected regardless of their differences.

PROBLEM-BASED LEARNING

Engaging and Relevant Curriculum: United We Stand

Patrick Anderson and Eli Bates both taught classes on the American political system on the high school level. Both used the district-required standards-based curriculum on how America selects the presidential and vice presidential candidates for political parties. Patrick used the traditional stand-and-deliver method. Some students were alert. A few were not paying attention and tried to text message their friends, but Patrick caught them. Others wrote down some political notes, and still others tried to look attentive. The rest were totally unengaged. At the end of the unit the students took a conventional multiple-choice, matching, true/false, and fill-in-the-blanks test to assess their content knowledge. Test results were mixed. As usual, the high-achieving students did well. The rest of the class scored in direct proportion to their engagement in the content.

Eli took a different approach to teaching the same unit. He let the class divide into two fictional political parties. Each party was responsible for developing its own platform based on issues relevant to their high school. Each party separately nominated its own presidential and vice presidential candidates just as the major American political parties do theirs. While Patrick was instructing his class, Eli led the two parties in conducting their campaigns, staging mock political conventions, and holding a mock election. Upon completion students compiled small-group reports addressing what they had learned in terms of the same district-mandated standards. Collectively, Eli's students scored higher on knowledge obtained and continued to refer to the project as both fun and highly informative throughout the school year.

> **Think About It**
>
> 1. How did each of these educators demonstrate teacher leadership skills in regard to engaging and relevant curriculum delivery? Describe the differences.
>
> 2. In what additional ways could each educator have enhanced his teacher leadership skills while enhancing student learning?
>
> 3. Explain the importance of students' active engagement in learning to a teacher who believes the only way to teach is for the teacher to talk and students to listen at all times.
>
> 4. What impact, if any, does active student engagement have on student learning styles and students of differing ability levels?
>
> 5. Develop a plan by which Eli's class project could be expanded to include whole school learning while also incorporating community members.
>
> 6. Some oppose standards-based education on the premise that it places too much pressure on some students who are not developmentally ready. Do you agree? Support your answer.

Developmentally Appropriate Instructional Strategies: Never, Ever, Ever Again!

Tammie McWhorter was teaching a unit on state geography to her mixed-ability group of third graders. In order to better engage all students in topographic learning, she wanted the students to create salt dough maps of their state. In so doing, the students could tie their topographic and geographic knowledge to their kinetic senses. Tammie also thought a hands-on project was developmentally appropriate for 8- and 9-year-olds, most of whom had never seen other parts of the state, which included plains, mountains, and a coastline. After discussing the idea with her principal, Tammie asked the children to bring old shirts to wear on top of their clothes while they did the project. She brought the ingredients for the salt dough maps and newspapers to spread on the floor to help keep the classroom clean.

As all teachers know, even the best plans can fall apart. When they prepared the salt dough, they put too much water into the mix, so the dough did not stick together. To remedy that problem, they added more salt and flour. Because this took more time than planned, they had to rush dividing up the dough to begin making their maps. They quickly learned that the consistency of the salt dough was still not right to make mountains, plains, and the coast. What it was good enough for was making a real mess.

The principal heard about it right after school that day and before Tammie could get to her. The lead custodian came to complain about the huge mess in the classroom, even though Tammie was trying to clean it up at that very moment. Upon checking, the principal found a messy classroom and a very upset teacher. She was just trying to engage her students in a developmentally appropriate activity that would also be fun, Tammie wailed. She didn't understand how such a good idea could go so wrong.

Think About It

1. In what ways did, or did not, Tammie demonstrate leadership skills in dealing with this situation?

2. In what additional ways could Tammie have enhanced her teacher leadership skills regarding implementation of developmentally appropriate instructional strategies?

3. What other things could Tammie have done ahead of time to prevent such a disaster while still providing an engaging learning experience?

4. Previous generations placed little focus on active student engagement. Teachers expected that students would sit quietly, listen, and learn. What has caused this change of focus and with what results? Include the role of societal and demographic changes in your response.

5. Is this change good or bad? Why or why not?

6. Describe a model plan for engaging community members in active learning classroom situations. Include strategies for enticing parents who are not otherwise actively involved or supportive of the school to become engaged.

Ongoing and Systematic Assessment: But He Can't Read!

When Vincent enrolled in Anita Walker's second-grade class, the standardized test records from his previous school showed him to be an excellent reader. However, it didn't take Anita long to learn that Vincent couldn't read at all. Anita conferenced with her principal about Vincent's lack of reading ability. Together they compared his cumulative records with his daily work. Something was wrong. Vincent's daily work was not aligned with his test scores. The principal came to Anita's class to observe Vincent's learning style, productivity, and interaction with the other children. She found him to be a pleasant, quiet little boy who could not read.

Soon after that, Anita and her principal met with an educational diagnostician to discuss Vincent's lack of literacy skills and what could be done to help him. The diagnostician was skeptical because his records clearly showed him to be an outstanding reader. She was convinced that further testing was not necessary and that the problem was in the classroom. Anita was offended and upset. She viewed this perspective as a lack of respect for her teaching and observation abilities. After further discussion, Anita and the principal convinced the diagnostician to observe Vincent in the classroom. After doing so the diagnostician had to admit that Anita appeared to be applying appropriate instructional strategies and that, indeed, Vincent gave no indication of being able to read, despite what his test scores said.

A conference was scheduled with Vincent's mother, and together they decided to test Vincent individually. When the results came in, Anita was not surprised. Vincent could not read. The Admission, Review, or Dismissal (ARD) committee wondered aloud how Vincent got the high reading scores he transferred from his previous school. The diagnostician made a personal trip to the previous campus to try to get to the bottom of the large discrepancy. No one claimed to know anything. Furthermore, Vincent's first-grade teacher was no longer with the district. Regardless, plans were put into place to get Vincent the help he needed to learn to read.

Think About It

1. In what ways did, or did not, Anita demonstrate teacher leadership skills?

2. In what additional ways could Anita have enhanced her teacher leadership skills?

3. Explain the concept of ongoing and systematic student assessment and its rationale and purposes.

4. Should a single set of test scores always be the benchmark for a student's academic performance? Why or why not?

5. In what ways could the family have been further involved in helping Vincent learn to read?

6. Develop and explain an intervention plan within your content and grade level to help a nonreading student improve his or her proficiency.

CONCLUSIONS

In this chapter we have looked at curriculum and instruction from a variety of perspectives. We have learned that teacher leaders go far beyond the basic requirements of classroom instruction to meet the needs of each student. Teacher leaders individualize teaching as much as possible in diverse classrooms. They respond to the varying needs of students and modify their curriculum and instructional strategies to meet those needs.

Teacher leaders provide relevant curriculum that has meaning in the students' daily lives. They use instructional strategies that are engaging, interesting, and even fun for students through projects, labs, cooperative learning, and many hands-on endeavors. Finally, teacher leaders are continually formally and informally assessing and measuring student progress toward their learning goals. If progress is not being made, a teacher leader researches and digs and does not give up until he or she determines the cause of the problem. Then the teacher leader works with others in the learning community, inside and outside the school itself, to come up with a plan to facilitate success for the student.

This may all sound idealistic. Well, it is. On the other hand, if we do not like idealistic scenarios, look around. There is plenty of illiteracy, cruelty, and violence to go around. Do you like your local and world conditions today? No? Then we need to do something about them. Ignoring or accepting that some students are not acting or learning in an acceptable manner will have a lasting impact on individuals, families, society, and our nation. Therefore, it is up to teacher leaders to be exactly that, leaders, in not accepting the status quo and not allowing anyone around us to accept mediocrity, either. Teacher leaders seek to move forward, to address whatever problems they find. That is what our vision of success is all about. Teacher leaders are the footsoldiers in the war against illiteracy and lack of education for the masses. Take a stand. Move forward. Conquer illiteracy and lack of educational opportunity in your world.

IT'S UP TO YOU

1. Describe the differences between curriculum and instruction in relation to teacher leadership and describe how each can be assessed.

2. Illustrate the role of technology for student learning today.

3. Explain and clarify the role of collaboration in teacher leadership and effectiveness.

4. A new teacher is confused about the distinction between learner-centered and traditional classrooms. In your role as mentor, explain the differences, provide examples, and describe a learner-centered lesson you could invite the new teacher to watch you implement.

5. The use of multiple sources of data for student assessment is important in a learner-centered classroom. Develop a teaching plan with objectives on a concept of your choice. Explain several types of appropriate assessments to meet the varying learning styles of various students.

6. Explain the role of risk taking in teacher leadership to enhance student learning. Provide examples.

A teacher leader can enhance systematic school improvement by . . .

- Seeking to improve instruction through a variety of methods, including personally modeling lessons for other teachers
- Surveying faculty and staff for their interests and needs in regard to improving curriculum and instruction
- Writing a curriculum that is aligned with local or state standards
- Collaborating in schoolwide or grade-level teams for curriculum support
- Facilitating vertical and horizontal alignment across the campus that is of practical value to educators in classrooms
- Actively engaging in districtwide curricular content scope and sequencing
- Promoting accountability among peers so that each instructor is teaching in developmentally appropriate ways
- Modeling and encouraging best instructional practices and cooperative learning to accommodate the learning styles of all students
- Modeling and encouraging actively engaged student learning rather than lectures where learners are expected to "sit and get"
- Facilitating best instructional practices for other teachers through mentoring and team planning
- Exhibiting leadership by helping teachers make time to plan and conference during the school day
- Conducting need assessments for new programs
- Being alert to changing student needs and modifying the curriculum to meet those needs
- Meeting individual student needs by differentiating instruction all day, every day

Equity for All Learners

Yesterday's Classroom Is Not Coming Back

"The best executive is the one who has sense enough to pick good men to do what he wants done, and self-restraint to keep from meddling with them while they do it."

—Theodore Roosevelt

CRITICAL ISSUE: DIVERSITY AND MULTICULTURALISM

Equal is not always equitable. The entire issue of equity is directly tied to ethics and morality. Often things must be reduced to their simplest form for people to understand them. We are going to do exactly that in reference to the distinction between equality and equity.

Let's look at the example of modifying student assignments and assessments for appropriately identified students with learning disabilities. Some people insist that if one child must do 20 long division problems, then every child must successfully complete the same 20 long division problems to the same standard. What one child must do, all children must do. They fail to take into consideration the multiple learning styles and differences between all humans. They think we should treat all students exactly the same.

Yet these same people would think it absurd to expect a student with a broken leg to run the 50-yard dash in order to pass a physical education course. Few would think that if a student cannot run the 50-yard dash, crutches and all, in a specified time period, he or she should fail. Most people would agree that a student with a broken leg should be given a different assignment and should not fail the course because of an injury. Thus, the student should receive a modified assignment.

Figure 6.1 shows that today we have students everywhere who have academic broken legs. For them, equal is not equitable. They need modified assignments.

Figure 6.1   Academic Broken Leg

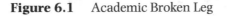

**Can This
Student Run?**

**Is This Student
Puzzled?**

PHILOSOPHICAL FRAMEWORK

Our society is changing in front of our very eyes. We have students in schools from multiple countries whose native tongue is not English. These students may or may not have learned to speak English yet. Although English is certainly not the only important language spoken in America, it is often necessary for effective communication in multiple settings. We also have students whose religions and customs seem different from what has previously been common. We even have students with physical and learning disabilities that precluded a public school education not long ago.

Yet today we teach all of them and do it very well. Furthermore, as teachers we want to do exactly that. Under the No Child Left Behind Act

Figure 6.2 Identifying and Respecting the Common Ground

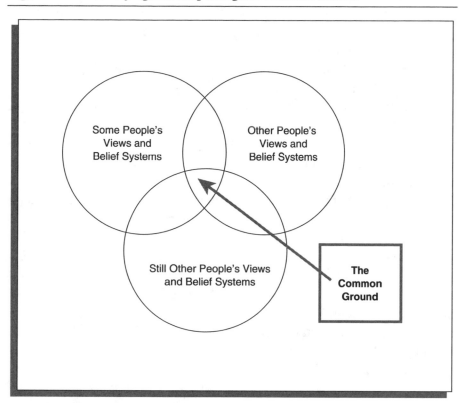

and many state and local testing systems, the performance of students by disaggregated subgroups is critically important to school and district performance ratings.

So what are teacher leaders supposed to do to address the needs of students in this diverse society in an equitable way? How are teacher leaders and others in a varied learning community supposed to bring diverse factions with drastically different perspectives together? In short, how are we supposed to help everyone achieve a common vision, generate success in its multiple forms, and create a learning community ripe with mutual respect and appreciation? A good place to start is by working collaboratively and respectfully to identify basic principles on which we can all agree. Figure 6.2 illustrates this common ground.

Identifying and Respecting the Common Ground

There are still educators who long for the "good old days" when students sat in straight rows, did exactly what you told them to do, and did it with nice manners. These students looked almost identical, and all came from families with similar belief systems. Educators who long for yesterday's classrooms believe that teaching back then was easy.

But I have a huge surprise for them. Yesterday's classrooms are not coming back. Nor should they return. Today's society is richer and fuller for the diversity and multiple cultures that we have. America has long been known as a melting pot, but we really are more of a mixed fruit salad than a casserole. In a casserole you take several different types of foods, cook them together in varying proportions, and end up with an entirely different entity. That is not what we should be trying to accomplish in our schools. We should not be trying to turn everyone into carbon copies of ourselves, nor should we try to blend everyone so that our individual cultures are lost. We are more of a mixed fruit salad where the apples, strawberries, cantaloupes, and bananas retain their distinctiveness while coming together but taste better than they would have individually. Therefore, yesterday's classrooms are not coming back. We are aiming for much richer classrooms in their place.

Getting everyone to agree on that, or anything else, can be a challenge. When dealing with groups of people who agree on very little, it is important to stay calm, remain collegial, and do your best to encourage a nurturing environment where all views can be heard. Ground rules for meetings should be established with reminders that everyone should remain civil, treat each other with respect, and keep the focus on what is best for the students. This is the model to follow for any kind of conflict resolution, whether it is in regard to student mainstreaming issues, cultural differences, or what to call the holidays that surround what are commonly known as Christmas and New Year's.

From there the idea is to get everyone talking in a civil manner without irritating each other. The key is to keep reminding everyone that we do not have to agree on everything. What we do need to do is to keep talking until we can identify some ideas on which we can agree. That can take a while. These ideas everyone can agree on are the foundation on which you will build the future.

Accepting and Appreciating Learning and Societal Differences

Schools are microcosms of the society in which they exist; therefore, problems that manifest themselves in the community will be reflected inside the school. Because students come from a cross-section of races, cultures, and belief systems, schools are an excellent place to bring people together so they can get to know each other personally. In so doing we can learn about cultures and beliefs that are different from our own while nurturing friendships between others to prepare our next generation of leaders.

Students learn in many different ways regardless of race, culture, or economic background. Some are visual learners, and others are auditory. Some are tactile-kinetic and learn best by doing things with their hands or bodies. Others learn best in interactive small-group settings, and others prefer to study independently. There are students who learn quickly and then bore easily. Some need to have things repeated or retaught in a different manner. Still others struggle with basic literacy skills while also being creative thinkers and writers. In other words, every student is different. Yet all of these students could be in the same classroom.

Learning to accept and appreciate students with learning differences can be difficult for both teachers and parents, especially if a physical or learning disability is profound. Teacher leaders acknowledge this and are always empathic to the needs of the family. But empathic as they are, teacher leaders press forward to help students find their rightful and successful place in the classroom, campus, and society. Teacher leaders never encourage students to depart from the traditions or rituals of their culture or race. They encourage the students to use them as assets that they can present to the world to make it a richer, better place. The distinction here is to view differences as assets rather than detriments. As the teacher leads, the classroom and school will follow. What the teacher values, students will value. Therefore, it is critically important for teacher leaders to model a school philosophy and lifestyle inside and outside the campus where diversity of all kinds is valued, respected, and appreciated.

By modeling a philosophy and lifestyle that value the diversity of the school community, teacher leaders can lay the groundwork for collaboration to develop and reach a common vision of excellence for the school (Figure 6.3).

Working Together to Reach the Vision

Working together in a collegial culture and climate is essential to reaching the vision of any organization. This is particularly true in schools. It cannot happen without the significant input of teachers as leaders.

As I have stated several times, teacher leaders are the foot soldiers in the war against illiteracy. They work directly with students, parents, and all parts of the learning community. That is why they are so important. Teacher leaders are critical forces in bringing these components together to help the school and classroom reach its vision of excellence. Teacher leaders are the "first face" to all families because they are the ones working directly with the children. If teacher leaders do not support and wholeheartedly endorse the campus vision, it will be incredibly hard, if not impossible, to achieve it.

Figure 6.3 Working Together to Reach the Vision

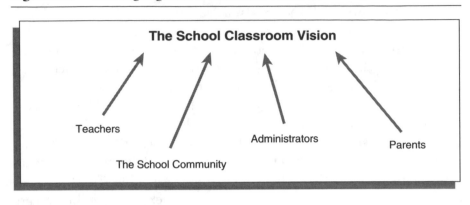

PROBLEM-BASED LEARNING

Identifying and Respecting the Common Ground: Choir, Band, Theater, Art, or Football?

Laity Charter High School is in the midst of a finance and culture war between those who want to expand the athletic program and those who want to expand the school arts programs. Each group has its own compelling reasons for supporting its own programs and reasons why they feel the other program is less important. Teachers and coaches from both groups are actively engaged in the discussion, with sometimes hot-tempered rhetoric. Neither group wants to give an inch.

At the same time, students in Bill Gilbert's honors American history class are analyzing reasons behind America's entrance into World War II. As highly intelligent teenagers, they discussed why there was a conflict at all, why Hitler could not be contained, and other problems that led to the beginning of the war before America got involved. Finally, one student wondered aloud why the countries involved could not come to a common ground and avert a war completely. "Good analysis," said Bill, wishing it really could have been that easy.

Later in the day, while eating lunch with a group of other teachers, Bill brought up the class discussion and the student's comment about finding a common ground. "Wouldn't it be great if we could come up with a common ground for the big argument going on right now between athletics and the fine arts people?" he wondered. "It sure would," they all agreed. Finding a common ground on which everyone could agree would be beneficial to the vision and mission of the school and certainly improve the tense campus culture and climate.

But who would or could facilitate getting appropriate stakeholders to come together to find this common ground? Campus and district administrators had already become battle scarred and weary. They knew they were going to have to make a difficult decision that would anger much of the school community regardless of what the decision was. "Maybe we should be the ones to try to pull people together," said another teacher during lunch. "Maybe we are the ones who need to step up to the plate. Our programs are not the ones under fire. We have no vested interest in which way this is resolved, can keep our personal feelings to ourselves, and can facilitate good communication and peace making. What do the rest of you think?"

Think About It

1. How did these campus teachers demonstrate leadership skills?

2. In what ways could the teachers enhance their own professionalism and development to improve problem solving and consensus building on their campus in this situation?

3. Is it a good idea for a group of teachers to take leadership in facilitating finding a common ground among people who have completely opposite opinions? Why or why not?

4. How could teacher leaders such as these devise a communication plan? What steps would they need to take? What support systems would they need?

5. Should teachers who are not in the athletic or fine arts departments get involved in finance and policy issues such as these? Why or why not? Support your answer.

6. Explain the benefits of finding a common ground for each of the entities involved and for the school, district, and greater school community.

Accepting and Appreciating Learning and Societal Differences: "I Don't Want My Kid Reading This!"

Teachers at Linda N. Townzen Middle School were caught in an attack by those who thought specific books should be removed from the reading list and the school library. These included such classics as *Huckleberry Finn* and *Catcher in the Rye*. Those opposed to the books thought they included offensive language and offensive stereotypes. Supporters of the books cited the students' need to be exposed to multiple genres and the basic classics of American literature and the rights of Americans to freedom of the press. They also recalled book burning as a part of historical censorship and strongly recommended against repeating the cycle.

The English teachers at Townzen were caught in the middle of the controversy because it was primarily their reading lists that were under attack. Some teachers thought it was easier to comply by removing the books until the controversy blew over and then reinstating them. They said there were equally good classics that could temporarily replace the ones under attack. Others adamantly refused, saying they were defending the principle of freedom of speech.

The teachers were perplexed as how to resolve the issue. They knew they were dealing with a changing society of acceptable and unacceptable behaviors and that these changes were reflected in the school. In their case, they were also reflected in their reading and library lists. "It's amazing," they mused. "Some of society is getting more open minded than ever before. Yet other parts of society are going in the exact opposite direction. How are we supposed to meet the needs of our students while also trying to get parents and community members to accept and appreciate not just learning differences but changes in society?" They credited the king from the musical *The King and I* as he also tried to address world changes and their effects in his own kingdom by saying the whole thing was a "puzzlement." The Townzen teachers firmly agreed.

Think About It

1. In what ways could the English teachers use leadership skills to address this controversial topic?

2. In what ways could the English teachers subsequently enhance their own leadership development by working with others on the importance of accepting and appreciating differences of opinion?

3. What could the teachers do to help the conflicting groups find common ground on this emotionally charged topic?

4. How could the teachers assure parents and others that reading and teaching from a given source do not necessarily endorse the concepts therein?

5. Explain the concept of censorship and ways teacher leaders could address it.

6. How can teacher leaders endorse and support equity of learning and societal differences without letting personal sentiment interfere with their communication skills and leadership development?

Working Together to Reach the Vision: Together We Build

Teachers at Melda Cole Ward Elementary School were committed to academic excellence for every student regardless of background, income, race, or academic level. They were determined to do everything they could do within the bounds of ethics and reason to provide a high-quality education for each child.

Working closely with the principal, teachers took the leadership responsibility to work with parents, churches, civic groups, social service agencies, local philanthropies, and other community entities to get everything the students needed to be successful. Whether the children needed school supplies, tennis shoes, or eyeglasses, the teachers worked solidly together with the community to ensure that all needs were met.

The same was true for intangible items such as academic success. Parents were actively solicited for everything from helping with art and music, to being guest speakers on any number of content issues, and to menial tasks such as making copies. Teacher leaders also approached the local Senior Citizens' Center to ask for volunteers to do tasks as simple as listening to a child read or going over math facts. The senior citizens who volunteered said the time they spent on campus was among the most rewarding that they had spent all week. The student benefits were also obvious because those who had no adults at home to listen to them read now had someone who did so and who took an interest in them as people.

The Melda Cole Ward teachers spent regular time together brainstorming additional ways to ensure student success in each life arena. They did not consider groups of students as belonging to a single teacher but considered every child's success to depend on all of them collectively. In this way, ownership in each student was spread across all teachers. The teacher leaders' unrelenting attitude and commitment to a common vision led to unprecedented student success at Melda Cole Ward Elementary School.

Think About It

1. How did teachers at Melda Cole Ward demonstrate leadership skills?

2. In what ways did or could the teachers enhance their own professionalism by working in a united and collective manner to ensure student success inside classrooms?

(Continued)

(Continued)

3. Explain the importance of teachers and other entities working together to achieve a common vision or mission.

4. Is it possible for teachers in schools of varying sizes to make a commitment to the success of every child? Why or why not?

5. Some students are "turned off" and do not want to participate in any group activity, including academics. What can teacher leaders do to turn these students on to academic and life success?

6. Explain creative techniques teachers from various grade levels can use with students from other classes to help them succeed academically in nontraditional ways.

CONCLUSIONS

It is up to teacher leaders to bridge the gaps between all forms of diversity and multiculturalism in society today. They have an advantage in reaching families and pulling people with vastly different perspectives together on behalf of their students. First, teacher leaders can help parents and other community members identify and respect a common ground on which they can all agree and focus on what is best for the children. Teacher leaders also serve as role models for others inside and outside the campus in accepting and appreciating learning and societal differences. As the teacher leads, others will follow. Finally, teacher leaders pull everyone together to reach the campus and classroom vision of excellence for all learners for a united, literate, free, and democratic society.

IT'S UP TO YOU

1. How can teachers be campus and community leaders in producing equality and equity to meet the needs of students of different races, genders, religions, and learning styles?

2. Meeting the academic needs of each student in every classroom can be exceedingly difficult, particularly when ability levels cover a wide range. In these situations, what can teacher leaders do to keep all students engaged while addressing content on vastly different levels for other students?

3. Many schools and communities have hot-button issues. In what ways can teacher leaders provide equity to all students when strong

sentiment and tempers within the school and the community are involved?

4. Each student comes to school from a particular home and societal environment. Whereas some students have strong home support systems, others do not. Explain ways a teacher leader can work with families to encourage students and provide necessary skills for parents to reinforce and help their children succeed academically and in life.

5. Describe a model by which classroom teachers can provide equity of educational opportunity for each student while staying within a school budget.

6. Will America have true equity in the public schools within the foreseeable future? Why or why not?

A teacher leader can enhance systematic school improvement by . . .

- Proving significant input on all distinctive programs, such as special education, reading recovery, content mastery, and other remedial or gifted programs
- Tutoring struggling students
- Demonstrating high expectations for all students, including those who are currently functioning below grade level
- Modeling equitable practices, including student success teams, small counseling groups, honor patrols, peer buddies, and peer mediation
- Initiating opportunities for all students to benefit from higher-level thinking skills such as through reading and math competitions, subject matter clubs, and ample opportunities for every student to participate in music and other fine arts programs
- Leading efforts to get specific feedback from other faculty and staff on needed areas of improvement and providing suggestions that would allow them to feel empowered and supported in all areas, including student behavior management
- Modeling and encouraging others to participate in multicultural activities that do more than coincide with holidays
- Reading and implementing ideas from culturally diverse texts
- Appreciating and celebrating cultural differences
- Encouraging students from different cultures to talk about their traditions, rituals, and ways
- Inviting community members from diverse backgrounds to visit the school and talk about their cultures and providing opportunities for

students and faculty to interact and have conversations with the guests

- Following news events from around the world and integrating them into classroom, campus, and extracurricular activities
- Providing opportunities for students to be involved in campus and classroom decision-making processes, as appropriate
- Analyzing instructional materials to ensure they represent diversity from all segments of society
- Reviewing all programs in a systematic manner to make sure they are meeting the diverse learning abilities and styles represented on the campus
- Learning and demonstrating that even as adults we should get along well with others

7
Effective Communication in Today's Schools and Society

It's Not What You Say, It's How You Say It

"A leader is a dealer in hope."

—Napoleon Bonaparte

CRITICAL ISSUE: COMMUNICATION

Maria Contaras was a department head in a large high school. She was highly intelligent and stayed on top of all the things necessary for her academic field, departmental budget, and myriad forms of paperwork.

However, Maria was not the success you might think she would be because she did not always act in a professional manner. She treated people poorly and generally gave an impression that she was smarter and more important than anyone else. Yet it was hard to complain to administrators about her behaviors because it was not *what* she said to other people but *how* she said it. Her tone and nonverbal communication gave the impression that dealing with mere mortals was beneath her self-appointed, highly esteemed rank in life. But when subordinates or parents complained, she was the voice of innocence. They could agree on what she said. The distinction was in how she said it. In short, Maria had extremely poor communication skills that kept her from being a true teacher leader.

PHILOSOPHICAL FRAMEWORK

A strong case can be made that teaching is a communicative art. The distinction for teacher leaders is the way in which they use communication skills on the behalf of students. Teacher leaders role model and place emphasis on providing students with the oral, written, and technological skills they need to present their ideas clearly and coherently. They encourage students to be communicative, to think creatively and collaboratively within groups, and to support each other in the process. In like manner, teacher leaders encourage risk taking among students as they express and support their ideas in a safe and nurturing environment. Most of all, teacher leaders use their own communication skills to advocate for all students by using every available resource in the school community.

Figure 7.1   Effective Active Listening Skills

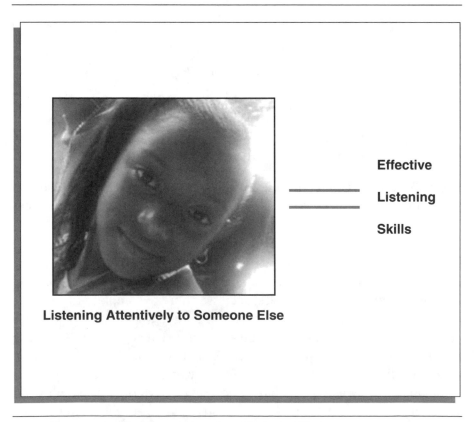

Source: Photo reprinted with permission from Kimberly Miller.

Figure 7.2   Noneffective Listening Skills

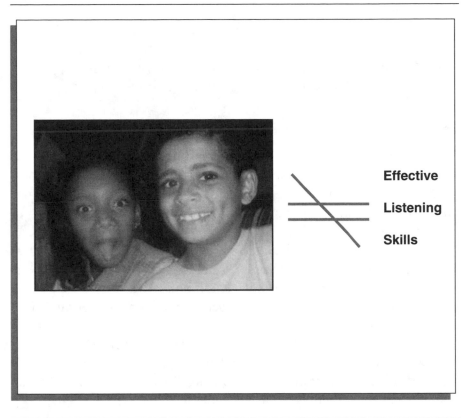

Source: Photo reprinted with permission from Kimberly Miller.

Active Listening Before Speaking

Listening effectively is an essential communication skill (Figure 7.1). Some people may think they are listening, as in Figure 7.2, yet they are not. They are actually thinking about something else while the other person is attempting to talk to them. This is not active or effective listening.

Before we can be heard, we must listen. It is human nature to want to get your two cents in. However, as teacher leaders we must bite our tongues and learn to actively listen before speaking. To actively listen means to really concentrate on what the other person is saying and the intent behind what he or she is trying to communicate. Stephen Covey (1990) expresses it well when he says we must seek first to understand. Listening to hear where the other person is coming from instead of thinking about what you are going to say next, before the person has even stopped speaking, is seeking first to understand that person's perspective. This is not to say that you have to agree with it or even think that it makes any sense. But if you can analytically interpret what the person is really trying to say, you can phrase your responses accordingly and spare everyone a lot of conflict and grief.

That does not mean it is easy to bite your tongue. Most of the time this is difficult. However, for teacher leaders actively listening to pupils, students, other teachers, parents, administrators, and everyone else in the world is a habit worth cultivating.

The Wonderful Power of Language

Language is so powerful. Who has not been moved by a passionate speaker, teacher, politician, activist, or anyone else who is strongly committed to a cause? How do these individuals do this? Through a combination of enthusiasm, commitment, and the effective use of language to promote their cause.

Our cause is educating students to fulfill their future roles as leaders in a freer and more democratic global society. For this we are investing our lives, careers, and passion for others. This is our cause. It is our hill worth dying on. It is what motivates us to work hard, work harder, and then work harder still until we think we are going to drop from exhaustion. It motivates us to get up in the morning when we are tired. It challenges us to work individually with every student, including the ones who don't seem to care whether they learn. Those are the ones we work with the hardest. This is what being a teacher leader is about. It is never giving up on anyone, using whatever positive tools we have to motivate and encourage students to learn, and savoring, treasuring, and appreciating the wonderful power of the oral and written word.

Teacher leaders can also use the power of language as they teach the fine arts. Who could ever see Michelangelo's fabulous sculpture of David and not be moved by the power of the statue? Who could ever see Leonardo da Vinci's angels in the Sistine Chapel and not be awed by the language of his paintings? And who has ever heard Handel's "Hallelujah Chorus" performed by any choir and not been moved to stand and marvel at the tradition and sheer majesty of the music? All of these fine arts venues and more are examples of the marvelous power of language. The arts are just a different kind of language, actually a more universal language, than the spoken word. For many, many students the fine arts are their own unique form of self-expression. They are also used extensively in various forms of therapy. Teacher leaders can use the power of the language of the arts in the classroom as another tool to meet the needs of every student.

A last form of language that is not commonly thought of as a language is perfectly described in a song Sandy Patty recorded. She sang,

Figure 7.3   The Public's Right to Know

Beleaguered,
Frustrated
Educator

"Love in any language fluently spoken here." She is right! In every school, in every classroom, in every home, the best teacher leaders are leading with love, which is fluently spoken through actions even more than words (Hoyle, 2001; Pellicer, 2003). People can say anything, but their actions show their true heart and intent.

The Public's Basic Right to Know

The public has a right to know what is going on at the school and in your classroom. That right has limits, of course (Figure 7.3). Parents do not have the right to see tests before they are given. They do not have the right to know personal information about other students, or at least not to hear it from the teacher. The right to confidentiality is very important.

However, parents do have a right to know the regular, day-to-day things that are occurring on campus. Furthermore, they have a right to be actively solicited to participate in those activities as an integral part of the school community. In order for that to occur, we as teachers must communicate with them in a regular, clear, and systematic manner in ways they can understand. If some parents do not speak English and we do not know their language, it is our responsibility to find a way, via an interpreter or whatever, to keep parents abreast of the status of their child's educational progress, to make them aware of things taking place at school, and to encourage their involvement as an important part of their child's education.

PROBLEM-BASED LEARNING

Active Listening Before Speaking: Growing Pains

Brandon and Ben were vocational teachers in Pedernales School District, which was a district in transition. For generations the district land area had been primarily agricultural. However, in the last several years the commerce and demographics of the district had begun to change. Several small industries had opened. This had spawned the growth of additional small businesses, which supported the industries. In addition, because of well-known problems in a much larger district nearby, many families were relocating to Pedernales in search of a smaller, safer, and more cohesive school environment.

Thus, Pedernales was experiencing growth pains from conflicting forces. Whereas some wanted to retain a small school atmosphere, others equally strongly thought it was time for the district to "grow up" in academic course offerings and extracurricular and cocurricular activities.

That's where teacher leaders Brandon and Ben got involved. For years the district had had an active, well-known, and quite well-respected agricultural department with a large number of students heavily involved in Future Farmers of America (FFA). Each year Pedernales students competed in and won state University Interscholastic League competitions. This did not happen year after year without the significant contributions of teacher leaders such as Brandon and Ben, who went beyond the call of duty training and helping their students prepare, compete, and achieve.

But many of the new people in town thought this type of activity was useless because their children were not going to grow up to be farmers. Offended, others responded that farmers are the backbone of our nation. Still others chimed in to remind everyone that there is more to FFA than raising cows and pigs. There are multiple leadership development activities as well as training for students in business, marketing, radio programming, debate, and other arenas. Therefore, they considered FFA an important activity that should remain available for all students who wanted to participate.

So the debate continued until it landed in the school board's lap because of budget problems caused by the state's public school financing formula, which was in chaos. Some thought district financial problems could be alleviated by the elimination of FFA and vocational education. Others were appalled at the idea and encouraged the school board to look elsewhere for budget cuts. Brandon and Ben were worried that the programs they had spent their careers developing were about to disappear.

Think About It

1. In what ways have Brandon and Ben shown teacher leadership skills, if any?

2. In what ways could Brandon, Ben, and other teachers enhance their communication skills on behalf of the FFA to show their alignment with the campus and district missions?

3. Should the agricultural teachers be involved in decision making about the future of the vocational program even though it is a policy and a budget decision that will be addressed by the school board? Support your response.

4. In what ways could better communication be used to create active listening and discussion between people who feel differently on this and other difficult issues by a growing district experiencing transitional pains?

5. In what ways can teacher leaders enhance, nurture, and sustain open communication involving active listening and collaboration on complex issues?

6. Compare and contrast the role of teacher leaders with that of administrators in facilitating open and active communication in the school community.

The Wonderful Power of Language: To Communicate or Not to Communicate?

Maggie was a born communicator. It had been said that she could sell anyone anything. When she chose to become a teacher, she felt she had found her niche. Indeed, it appeared that she had. She was successful in the classroom, in her relationships with students, and among her peers and administrators. As time went by she continued to teach and also got her master's degree at night from a nearby university. Maggie's life goal was to be a great teacher leader. She had no plans to become an administrator.

Not too long after she received her master's degree, the superintendent's office called and said Dr. Rollen wanted to see her.

On the appointed afternoon Maggie met with Dr. Rollen, who explained to her that the district was growing and strongly considering adding a central office position to deal mainly with the press. The primary responsibilities of this position would be to put the district's best foot forward in dealing with local newspapers, television, and radio and keeping up the district's Web site. Maggie had been mentioned as an excellent candidate for this position. As a natural communicator Maggie was known for using the power of language to help get the things she needed for her students to succeed. Dr. Rollen thought these were the same positive attributes needed for the potential new public relations position. Although she did not ask Maggie to make a decision on the spot, she did ask Maggie to strongly consider it and get back to her in the next few days.

Think About It

1. In what ways had, or had not, Maggie previously demonstrated leadership skills?

2. Explain how word choice, inflection, delivery, and other language skills can be important components in communicating and fulfilling a campus mission.

3. Provide examples in which the use of language has worked in both a positive and a negative manner and explain the results in each case.

4. How can language be used as a tool in problem solving and consensus building?

5. Should Maggie accept the potential public relations job? Why or why not?

6. Would Maggie no longer be a teacher leader if she stepped out of the classroom to assume another role in the district? Explain your response.

The Public's Basic Right to Know: Show Choir or No Choir?

Few would dispute that the public has every right to know how their money is being spent in any tax-supported organization. But at Horseshoe Bend High School it was becoming unclear where the public's right to know ends and plain old nosiness begins.

Jana Bearden had been directing the highly selective Show Choir at Horseshoe Bend High School for 7 years with great success. Jana developed and implemented the choir herself as an extension of the school vision of reaching, engaging, and extending the talents of every student.

Although the school had several other choirs, the Show Choir was an extracurricular group that performed choreographed popular songs and showtunes and was in high demand for school and civic performances. In the 7 years Jana had been directing the Show Choir, the group had won many awards. Each year more students auditioned. Membership in the choir had become highly selective.

This year the choir had been invited to perform in a prestigious competition for top show choirs in the nation. The competition was to be held at Disney World during spring break so the students would not miss any school days. Jana and the students were very excited about being selected. They received permission from their principal, superintendent, and school board to participate if they raised the money themselves, no tax dollars were spent, and appropriate supervision was obtained.

Multiple fundraising events were held, such as car washes, a musical spaghetti dinner in the school cafeteria, a huge civic garage sale, and a "Rent a Choir Member" campaign. All proceeds were deposited in a specific fund for the Disney World trip. The funds were to be divided equally among all students who participated in the activities. Scrupulous records were kept by both Jana and parent volunteers.

Because of the amount of publicity around town that the Show Choir was getting for its multiple fundraisers, one citizen decided he wanted to see all their financial records. He decided it was his personal mission to make sure the funds were being used for what they were supposed to be used for. At first Jana and the parent volunteers, who included a certified public accountant, gave him copies of everything he asked for. But as time went by, the man became a genuine nuisance. He asked for the same things over and over, questioned every expenditure, and continuously claimed money was being misspent when it was not. "At what point," Jana asked her principal, "can we just tell him that enough is enough? We are exhausted from having to waste large amounts of time, energy, and pure frustration on him!"

Think About It

1. In what ways did, or did not, Jana demonstrate leadership skills in directing the Show Choir and planning the Disney World trip?

2. In what ways could Jana enhance her skills as a teacher leader in regard to articulating the campus mission and that of the Show Choir to generate even greater school and community support?

(Continued)

(Continued)

3. Because the Show Choir was an extracurricular activity, was Jana required to disclose their financial records? Why or why not?

4. How can teacher leaders use fine arts programs to enhance individual learning styles and differences between students?

5. Weigh the pros and cons of Jana, or one of the most actively involved parent volunteers, politely letting the citizen know that he has become a nuisance and asking him to cease and desist.

6. In what respectful ways could Jana use her communication skills as a teacher leader to redirect the citizen's energies for the benefit of the Show Choir?

CONCLUSIONS

Our communication skills are critical to our success as teacher leaders. They are the tools we use to articulate the vision of our campus and our classroom. They are also the tools we use to transfer knowledge to students. The power of language in all its forms, including the arts, has been vital in communicating thoughts, philosophies, drama, and emotions from prehistoric times to the present. Our legacy to generations to come will be carried forth in the way we communicate with each other today. For this to occur we must learn to actively listen to each other and analyze what others are trying to communicate before jumping in to tell them what we want to say. Seek first to understand the other person's point of view. Even if you do not agree with it, which you may not, at least try to understand why the other person feels the way he or she does. This will be the first step in consensus building and bringing varied points of view together in an increasingly diverse and multicultural society.

IT'S UP TO YOU

1. Identify and elaborate on ways a teacher leader can effectively communicate the mission of the school in the neighborhood and district.

2. Brainstorm and describe innovative and effective strategies teacher leaders can use to communicate information to students, families, and the campus.

3. How does the communication system between teacher leaders and their followers function? How can it be improved?

4. Identify and describe effective professional and interpersonal communication skills that teacher leaders must use to maximize classroom and campus productivity.

5. Many schools have at least a few parents who do not seem to want to be happy with anything occurring on campus. What proactive techniques can a teacher leader use to address this situation?

6. In what ways can a teacher leader communicate and serve as an advocate for the needs of each student?

A teacher leader can enhance
systematic school improvement by . . .

- Providing written memos, e-mail communications, the school newspaper, a regularly updated campus Web site, and announcements about all campus activities, including parent conferences
- Routinely soliciting feedback from faculty and staff members on all issues affecting the campus and learning environment
- Consistently demonstrating openness to other people's ideas and input even if they do not seem reasonable at first
- Making sure that all parents are listened to and that their input is valued, particularly in regard to student discipline and complaints
- Taking an active role in brainstorming, decision making, and implementation of ways to improve all communication arenas
- Planning and implementing general faculty, grade-level, and departmental meetings in a systematic manner
- As applicable, sending online communication with frequent reminders to parents and other community stakeholders interested in the success of students and the campus
- Holding regular personal conferences with parents, peers, auxiliary personnel, administrators, and others invested in the success of the students
- Ensuring that memos or other forms of communication for parent and community activities are sent well in advance and in the correct languages
- Providing information for an attractive, effective, and up-to-date school marquee
- Valuing and analyzing the input of all stakeholders, even if they seem crazy

Teacher Enhancement

If You're Standing Still, You're Moving Backwards

"I must follow the people. Am I not their leader?"

—Benjamin Disraeli

CRITICAL ISSUE: TEACHER PROFESSIONAL ENHANCEMENT AND DEVELOPMENT

A family of avid skiers looked forward to taking their 9-year-old daughter, Gracie, on her first ski trip. On their first day they signed Gracie up for ski lessons while attacking the more difficult slopes themselves.

When they picked Gracie up that afternoon they excitedly asked her how she liked learning to ski. To their vast surprise Gracie told them in terms only a 9-year-old could come up with that she did not like skiing at all! Because her parents loved to ski, they were surprised to learn their child apparently did not enjoy skiing one bit. But rather than trying to change her mind or chastising her for not enjoying it, her wise mother asked, "What did you not like about it, Gracie? How can we make it better?"

The number one leadership question in your career and in your life is, "How can we make it better?" It does not matter what the issue or the "it" is. To be continuously improving in any arena, we must all ask ourselves how we can make the situation and ourselves better. That is what teacher enhancement is all about: making ourselves better. How can we become

Figure 8.1 Good to Great Teacher Leaders

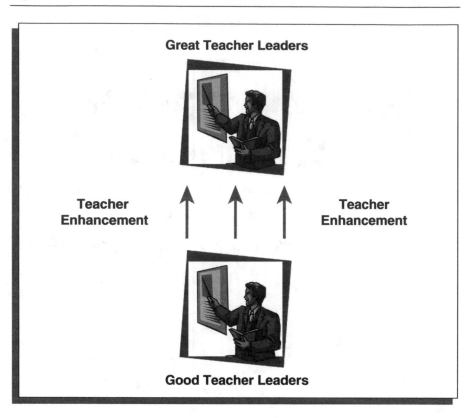

better teacher leaders? Citizen leaders? Contributing members of society? How can we lose weight, have enough money for a great vacation, or achieve world peace? The issue does not matter. As shown in Figure 8.1, making it better, or enhancing teacher leadership, is what counts.

PHILOSOPHICAL FRAMEWORK

It may sound paradoxical to say that if you are standing still, you are moving backwards, but it is not. Organizational gurus Tom Peters (1987) and Jim Collins (2001) have pointed out that one of the biggest obstacles to becoming a great organization is being a pretty good organization. In other words, organizations, including schools, can work hard to achieve specific goals and reach certain accomplishments, then tend to rest on their laurels with an, "Ah! We made it!" attitude when it happens. The next thing you know, they are no longer on the cutting edge. In fact, they have become what they worked so hard to not be: a merely good, not great, organization. Who wants to be ordinary? Who wants to work in an ordinary school or be an ordinary teacher? Certainly not us! We want to be teacher leaders who always set the example for others in how we lead our classrooms and campuses.

Using this same line of thought, good organizations never stop pressing forward to become even better (Collins, 2001; Peters, 1987). Schools, and classrooms themselves, are organizations. As teacher leaders we endeavor to never stop pursuing excellence, to never stop pushing ourselves and others to maximize what we can do to improve student learning, and to never, ever settle for being ordinary. Those who accept ordinary need to be recharged, to refuel their batteries, and to recognize that every child, in every school, in every classroom deserves the best we have. If we don't seize every opportunity for forward movement, we lose traction. We become the status quo. Others move ahead of us. Therefore, when we are not moving forward, we are losing ground, moving backwards. What teacher would want to feel as if someone else's students were receiving a better opportunity to learn than his or her own? This is not a competition between teachers, however. It is a quest to ensure that every student has optimal learning opportunities. This can happen only when we as teacher leaders take the time to reflect and look inside ourselves to become everything we possibly can be, professionally and personally. Taking time to think, reflect, and journal (Figure 8.2) is an important step in looking inside ourselves to discern who we really are, what we want to be, and how we plan to get there.

Looking to Your Future Through In-Depth Personal Assessment

Becoming a teacher leader is more than being a classroom expert. It is being a leader in all aspects of your life. It is impossible to separate the personal and professional aspects of who you are. What takes place in your personal life carries over into your professional life. That is why teachers who are undergoing great hardship or trauma, such as the critical illness of a family member, a death, or a divorce, cannot simply turn off the emotional parts of their lives when they walk into school. They may manage their emotions, but no one can turn them off completely.

For students the same is true. This is why we have student service programs, free and reduced-price lunch programs, counseling, and other programs to meet the needs of the whole child. Teachers are people, too. Everything about our lives affects our classroom performance regardless of how professional we try to be.

Although there are usually many people in our lives who are happy to tell us what they think we ought to do, think, believe, or react to, the only

Figure 8.2   In-Depth Personal Assessment

Source: Photo reprinted with permission from Elaine L. Wilmore.

person who can do this with any real impact is you. The only person who can truly look inside you to find out what brings you joy, fulfillment, and peace is you. There are many people and programs readily available to help you assess your strengths, weaknesses, and career choices, but for those who do not have the time or resources to undertake such a professional analysis, there is a much less expensive method any of us can benefit from. It does not cost any money and can be done in any location. At first, it seems simplistic. However, that definitely does not mean that it is easy. In fact, it is quite difficult if done properly. The more you put into it, as in anything else in life, the more you will get out of it.

I call it the Elaine Wilmore #1 Question for Improving Your Life and Leadership Skills. Are you ready? The #1 question to improve your life, leadership skills, or anything else is **"How can I make it better?"**

The "it" in "How can I make it better?" is generic. On the professional level "it" can be your classroom management skills, instructional strategies, relationships with other teachers and administrators, or student performance. On the personal level "it" can be time with your family, weight loss, health habits, exercise, or anything that will make you a happier, healthier, and more productive person. Remember, anything that helps to make you a better, happier, more fulfilled person is going to spill over into your classroom. Long-standing research in psychology and organizational leadership has shown that more fulfilled people usually are more productive in the workplace. Therefore, if learning to play the violin has been a long-standing dream in your life but you have never had the time or resources to learn to do it, now may be the time. If learning to play the violin is something that is going to bring you fulfillment and inner joy, don't cheat yourself of it by saying, "I don't have time," "I don't have a violin," or "I don't have any idea where to find a violin teacher, nor do I have the money to pay for one." Those are excuses. Make a list of your potential obstacles, and then brainstorm ways to overcome them. Some will work. Some won't. Keep trying till you find the exact ones that will work for you. Never stop until you fulfill your goals, and never give up on your dreams.

What gets measured gets done. Therefore, once you have your plan for learning to play the violin, losing weight, or increasing your effectiveness in teaching students of a different race or culture from your own, put it into place. Give it a timeline. Goals without deadlines are only dreams. Create a deadline for each step of your plan. When those dates come, assess how you are doing. Sometimes you will be doing really well. That's great. Give yourself a pat on the back.

Other times, you may not be making as much progress toward your goal at your deadline as you had hoped to see. In those cases, do not throw out the plan or the dream. Adjust it just as you would modify an instructional strategy that was not working for a student in your classroom. And remember the Socratic method of constantly searching for truth through questioning and introspection as you answer each question. The benefits you receive will be directly proportionate to the true analysis and intrinsic worth that you put into each response.

Steps in the Elaine Wilmore "How Can I Make It Better?" Model

Figure 8.3 illustrates the Elaine Wilmore "How Can I Make It Better?" Model.

Model for Personal and Professional Enhancement

1. Identify "it." Exactly what do you want to improve?

2. What are the things you will need to do to achieve this goal? For example, if you want to learn to play the violin, you would need to

Figure 8.3   How Can I Make It Better?

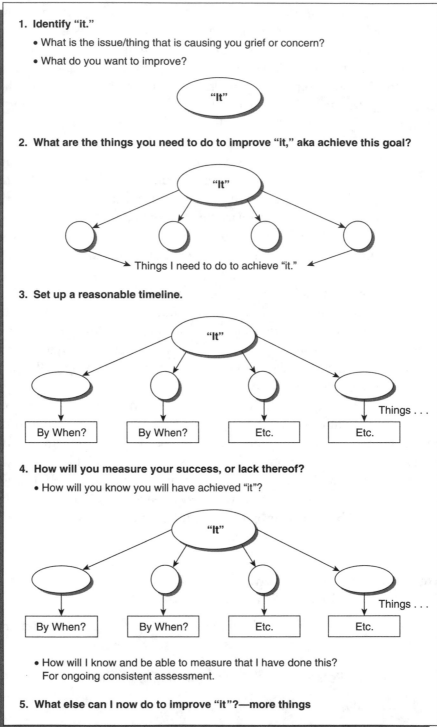

1. **Identify "it."**
   • What is the issue/thing that is causing you grief or concern?
   • What do you want to improve?

   "It"

2. **What are the things you need to do to improve "it," aka achieve this goal?**

   "It"

   Things I need to do to achieve "it."

3. **Set up a reasonable timeline.**

   "It"

   | By When? | By When? | Etc. | Etc. |

   Things . . .

4. **How will you measure your success, or lack thereof?**
   • How will you know you will have achieved "it"?

   "It"

   | By When? | By When? | Etc. | Etc. |

   Things . . .

   • How will I know and be able to measure that I have done this?
     For ongoing consistent assessment.

5. **What else can I now do to improve "it"?—more things**

- Get a violin.
- Find someone to teach you.
- Set up lesson times.
- Get the sheet music the teacher requests.
- Begin lessons.
- Practice.
- *Learn to play the violin!*

3. Set up a reasonable timeline. Remember, goals without deadlines are only dreams.

4. Determine how you will measure your success. How will you know that you are, indeed, learning to play the violin? Remember, what gets measured gets done.

5. Identify other things you may need to do to achieve your goal.

I told you earlier that this model is deceptively simple. The reason it is deceptively simple is that it is easy to throw a few thoughts together and say you have completed the process. But true growth comes only from in-depth personal and professional reflection that leads to reflective intro-spection, personal and professional assessment, and enhancement. You will reap benefits in direct proportion to the heart-wrenching probing you put into your deepest self to find what will really help you become the most fulfilled person and teacher leader you can be.

The beauty of this plan is that it is ambidextrous. It is equally user-friendly for both the "its" you identify to help you as a teacher leader in your school and classroom and the "its" you identify to help you become the best person you can be. The two go together. They are aligned. It can almost be said that you can't have one without the other, but there are always exceptions. I don't want you to be an exception. I want you to be the best person you can be as both a citizen and a teacher leader. Routinely ask yourself, "How can I make it better?" in each aspect of your life. Make it a habit. Never let a day go by without asking yourself this question in each arena of your life. The results will amaze you. Tiny things add up to big changes over time. They also will mean greater productivity and hap-piness for you and those around you.

The Intrinsic Need for Quiet, Reflection, and Recreation

Everyone has heard the old phrase, "I've got to get out of here." But have you ever said it and really, really meant it? Most of us have. There are times when we have given and given and given, and that's it. We've reached a physical and emotional brick wall. You're not actually ill. But

Figure 8.4   The Intrinsic Need for Quiet, Reflection, and Recreation

Source: Photo reprinted with permission from Elaine L. Wilmore.

you can't go on, and you do realize it. The truth is, you just plain need a break. You need time alone, solitude, and a physical and emotional release. You need stillness, peace, and quiet, and you need it *now.* Getting away, even briefly, to a quiet place of solitude and reflection can create just the right state of mind to help your body and soul relax, regroup, and reframe (Figure 8.4).

There is a difference between this kind of "soul fatigue" and routinely not wanting to get out of bed in the morning. Everyone is tired at times. Soul fatigue comes when your soul is empty. There is simply nothing left. You are so tired that you've lost every last bit of zest in all areas of your life. You are running on empty, fulfilling your responsibilities as best you can, but you are so worn out that nothing seems to matter. It's not long-term depression. It is soul fatigue, and something must be done about it.

That's where the part about getting out of here comes in. The location is not the issue. In fact, staying home and hiding from the world is a pretty good option. As long as you can be quiet, let your mind, heart, and soul rest, and be physically removed from the areas that have caused you to wear down so completely, the location is not the issue.

Going somewhere far from anything that vaguely resembles your personal reality is even better than staying home. It is amazing what one simple, quiet weekend staring at nothing and doing nothing can do for your soul. If it involves mountains, lakes, rivers, or the ocean, it's even better. There is something highly therapeutic about staring at the strength of mountains, the tranquility of water, or the lovely old gardens at a historic bed and breakfast. Losing yourself in nature is a strikingly good idea.

I can hear some of you now thinking you don't have time or money for a weekend, or even a weekday, away. I have a better question. Do you have time *not* to take some time away, be removed from the situation, and let your soul heal? As humans we all need times of quiet like this. You are not admitting defeat to the stress in your lifestyle. You are making a genuine effort to let your heart, mind, soul, and often even your brain have the time they need for the three *R*'s of personal enhancement:

- Regenerating
- Regrouping
- Reflecting

According to *Merriam Webster's Collegiate Dictionary, 11th Edition, to regenerate* means to become "spiritually reborn, renewed or restored, especially after a decline to a low or abject condition." When our souls are fatigued we are in a "low or abject condition" and truly need to be reborn, renewed, and restored. Likewise, *Webster's* says that *to regroup* means "to group again; reassemble or reorganize . . . to collect oneself, as after a loss or setback." There are times when all of us, even as superhuman teachers, need time to internally "group again" and "collect oneself, as after a loss or setback." Sometimes it does not even take a loss or setback. A teacher can be completely worn out after any intensely stressful situation such as state-or district-mandated high-stakes testing. Once those are over is an ideal time for us to collect ourselves, regroup, and let ourselves relax. Last, *Webster's* says *to reflect* means, "to think seriously; to contemplate." Everybody alive can benefit from serious contemplation or reflection on where they are in their lives, where they want to be, and what must happen to get them there. Therefore, all of the three *R*'s, regenerating, regrouping, and reflecting, are equally important to teacher enhancement.

Taking the time to do these things is not selfish. They are very, very good things. Anyone who does not understand this does not understand basic human needs. There is a limit to how much pressure, stress, and accommodation your body and mind can take. The critical issue is being able to discern when you have reached this level of soul fatigue and having the courage to do something about it. If that means taking a day off from school, then do it. Anything moral and reasonable that makes you a better you is a good thing. If you stay home and practice your violin all day and that makes you a calmer, rejuvenated you, it is a good day. Some call days away from campus for personal or professional enhancement "staff development." I call them necessary.

For many people sports, weight training, running, biking, swimming, and even aerobic walking or other things that involve active body motion help them relax, kick out tension, and get their act together for the future. The physical and emotional health benefits of exercise are well documented. All of us know this, but too many of us do not act on what we know. Reasons vary. The main excuse we hear and use is that we do not have time to exercise. Yet who cannot find as little as 15 minutes a day to walk around the block, up and down the halls of the school, on a treadmill, or around the campus or a football field track? Sure we can. It's a matter of priorities. For your health and for emotional stability and stress release, regular exercise is the thing to do. Exercise is a positive addiction. The more you do it, the more you want to do it. The most necessary step is the first step: getting started. Make the decision today and begin. Some addictions are good. Exercise is one of them.

The Role of Continuous Enhancement Through Reading, Research, and Professional Associations

In the end, regardless of how well our bodies and psyches are doing, we must be lifelong learners. To be teacher leaders, we cannot expect other people to be growing and learning around us while we sit back, not expanding our horizons as well. Teacher leaders are growing all the time. They are constantly asking themselves, "How can I teach and lead better? How can I make learning and life more successful for each of my students? How can I better teach the hard to teach? How can I better relate to students whose backgrounds are so different from my own? How can I have exceedingly high expectations for students who do not speak my language and don't understand a word I say?"

The answer is teacher enhancement, otherwise known as professional development with an edge (Figure 8.5). Teacher enhancement is about making all things better. If we want to improve student performance and

Figure 8.5   Teacher Enhancement

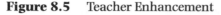

Teacher
Enhancement
————————
————————
Professional
Development
With an Edge

initiate change and educational reforms, we must also be looking to our own professional needs (Little, 1985). Our efforts to improve ourselves will be reflected in how well we can teach and work with students (Danielson, 2006). If our students are not being successful, let's figure out why. Let's tear apart multiple forms of assessment data to figure out where their individual strengths and weaknesses are, then plan our campus and personal growth activities around targeted ways to help specific students improve. If taking conversational Spanish classes through community education, or something similar, will help us be better able to communicate with our students and their families, we will do our best to sign up. If data indicate that our students have poor reading comprehension skills and we have done everything we know to do to help them, obviously this is an area for us to address. If anything we determine to be a weakness for our students is not a targeted need for our entire campus and is not being addressed through regular staff development, we will take it on as our personal cause. Find whatever you can do to enhance your own teaching skills in this area. Where or how you improve your skills is not the issue. Improving yourself so you can create success for students is the issue. Sometimes, in fact fairly often, this will mean stepping out on your own, seeking help through research, reading, consulting with others inside and outside your school and district, and attending conferences sponsored by your professional organizations, at a college or university, or at any type of regional service center. These can all be ways to target your own needs by assessing the weaknesses of your students.

Remember, the issue is not about you. The issue is about generating student success. If you think you have done everything within your control to help your students understand what they are reading, yet they still score poorly in reading comprehension, do not blame anyone. The Blame Game never solved anything. Get the help you need to do a better job. Doing it yourself while encouraging others to do likewise is teacher leadership. Do whatever you need to do to help your students succeed, and encourage anyone who will listen to do likewise. That is teacher leadership. That is growing as a professional. That is lifelong learning. You are successful when your students and those around you are successful. Until that happens, we are not done yet. Getting there is what teacher leadership is all about.

PROBLEM-BASED LEARNING

Looking to Your Future Through In-Depth Personal Assessment: Taking Time to Think About It

Hope Barnes was one of the best kindergarten teachers anyone in her area had ever known. She had a wonderful natural gift for communicating and establishing rapport with young children and their families. She was equally talented in mentoring other teachers and assisting them in their development as teacher leaders. As if all this weren't enough, Hope was frequently called on to be a speaker on early childhood issues in other school districts and through her professional organizations. Hope had no desire to become a principal or curriculum specialist. She was happy and fulfilled in her role as a kindergarten teacher.

One day, while she was doing a back-to-school inservice presentation to other teachers in a nearby district, it suddenly hit her that her walk was not matching her talk. There she was, encouraging others to look deep into themselves to find their true callings, to identify the things that brought them the most joy and fulfillment, and to get rid of all the rest. "Just because you can do something," Hope told them, "does not mean that you must do it." Yet wasn't that exactly what she was doing?

The thought struck her as so profound that she caught her breath. She knew that she was doing that very thing. She didn't have time to reflect on it right then because she was in the middle of the presentation. However, on the way home she gave it intense thought. Hope realized that being in the classroom working with young children was what brought her the most joy. Although she was good at all the other things she seemed to have allowed herself to be brought into, her real passion was teaching young children and watching them grow.

That night Hope discussed all this with her husband, who supported her soul searching and reflections completely. They realized that if she stopped doing the presentations and consulting, it would result in less income for their household. Therefore, it was important to Hope to make such decisions jointly with her husband. The two of them weighed their options and decisions over a period of time.

In the end, Hope met with her principal and told her that for the time being she wanted to focus all her energies on her classroom and would no longer be interested in doing external consulting and presentations. As further opportunities came her way, Hope told them the same thing. For this moment in her life, being a teacher leader of kindergarten students was what brought her the most fulfillment and contentment, so that was what she was going to be. Things could change at another time, but for now she was happy in Room 101 with a class full of 5-year-olds.

Think About It

1. How did Hope demonstrate introspective leadership skills?

2. In what ways could Hope continue to enhance her own professional development while focusing her time and energies on her students and classroom?

3. Was it selfish on Hope's part to not want to share her expertise with others outside her school?

4. Because she stopped her external consulting and presenting, would Hope no longer be a teacher leader? Why or why not?

5. When you look deep into yourself, what things bring you the most joy and fulfillment? What things are you currently busy with that do not bring you joy and fulfillment?

6. Develop a personal enrichment plan with a timeline in which you begin eliminating the things in your life that do not bring you fulfillment and focus on the things that do. Also focus on things you have always wished you had the time to do but have never done. Pick at least one and add it to your enrichment plan.

The Intrinsic Need for Quiet and Recreation: I've Just Got to Get Out of Here

Sparkle was a teacher who worked unbelievably hard. In addition to her school workday, she regularly worked nights and weekends, always looking for a better way to reach her often difficult-to-teach students. It wasn't that she didn't like to relax. It was that she thought she did not have time to sit back, unwind, and just have fun. She was always working on something.

Periodically her body would revolt, and she would get sick. But she always got well quickly, returned to work, and rapidly returned to her old habits of lots of work and very little rest. Family and friends often shook their heads and made comments about how driven and focused she was on helping her students. Privately, many of them wondered whether it was worth the toll it was taking on her physically and emotionally. Sparkle was always tired, always worn out. There were times when even she wondered whether it was worth it at all.

One winter day a friend passed her a flyer for a retreat being held that spring about 5 hours from where she lived, in a part of the state she really loved. The retreat was to focus on quiet, solitude, nature, and personal growth. Sparkle looked at it longingly and then looked at the dates. She sighed and wished she could go. But she knew she couldn't. There was no way she could be away from the school at that time. However, she didn't throw the flyer away. She simply tucked it away. From time to time she looked at the flyer. Each time she looked at it, she wished she could go. But each time, she realized it was not realistic and put the flyer away.

One day, when Sparkle was particularly tired, an emotional mess and near tears, her eyes again fell on the flyer. This time, instead of putting it away, she looked at the dates and her calendar. The more she thought about it, the more she really, really wanted to go. She talked to her family and principal and rearranged some important commitments. When the time came, she got in her car and drove 5 hours to a retreat where she didn't know a single person. Her heart told her it was the right thing to do.

And it fed her soul. The quiet, solitude, and hiking in the beauty of the hills were exactly what her mind and body needed. The speakers touched her heart. The time alone in an outdoor rocking chair, hammock, and wooden swing gave her occasions to think and reassess her values and life. By the time the retreat was over, Sparkle again cried. But this time they were tears of release. She did not want to leave the retreat center or the new friends she had made there. It wasn't that she did not want to return to her home, family, or job. It was that she didn't want to leave the retreat for fear of losing herself yet another time. She pledged to return again and to not lose sight of who she really was on the inside ever again.

Think About It

1. In your opinion, was it right or wrong for Sparkle to take time off for a retreat that did not have a direct educational purpose? Why or why not?

2. In what ways did the retreat probably enhance Sparkle's teacher leadership effectiveness?

3. What does time at a retreat center have to do with being a teacher or any other kind of leader?

4. When Sparkle cried and did not want to leave the retreat, what was her soul telling her?

5. Is it possible as a teacher leader to give too much of yourself, such that you lose your effectiveness? Explain your response.

6. What impact can a retreat or other time of quiet, reflective solitude have on your own life? What impact could this have on your teacher leadership effectiveness?

The Role of Continuous Enhancement Through Reading, Research, and Professional Associations: Bring It On!

When Lukka graduated from college and got his teaching certificate, he thought, "That's it. I never want to go into a college classroom or anywhere else where I'm expected to learn anything again. I am done!" Then he got a teaching job and learned that his education had just begun.

The first year of his teaching career Lukka learned quickly that there was more to teaching biology than standing, delivering, and conducting labs with students. Although the labs went pretty well, the time when he was directly teaching students left a lot to be desired. Students did not seem interested or engaged, and as much as he hated to admit it, he thought some of his students were writing notes to each other rather than taking notes on his stellar lectures.

Lukka knew he needed to improve his teaching strategies, or he would never become the master teacher he had previously thought he would easily become. Realizing his mistake, Lukka began talking to more experienced teachers, seeking their knowledge and input on better ways to engage his students in learning. He asked his principal for recommendations of additional things to read or conferences to attend so he could improve as a future teacher leader. To his pleasure, each person he spoke with was quite willing to help him find direction and also seemed pleased that he had sought input from them. In fact, several told him they were honored that he had solicited their thoughts. Lukka had been concerned that if he asked for help others would perceive him as weak. But the opposite happened. His principal and peers respected him for asking for help and for wanting to grow and improve as an educator.

Think About It

1. In what ways did, or did not, Lukka demonstrate progress toward becoming a teacher leader?

2. In what ways other than reading and attending conferences could Lukka improve his instructional strategies?

3. Was it presumptuous of Lukka to ask for help from others who had their own jobs to do?

4. In what ways could Lukka measure his improvement as a teacher leader?

5. In what ways could Lukka involve his students in enhancing classroom performance?

6. Take some time to evaluate your own teacher leadership performance. Identify your personal strengths and potential weaknesses. Describe specific ways you can improve your own skills as a teacher leader.

CONCLUSIONS

The enhancement of your skills as a teacher leader is essential to becoming the professional educator, as well as the person, that your students, family, and, yes, even you yourself, deserve. Although school districts may require you to attend inservice sessions, they cannot make you learn anything. You can sit there until the earth quakes, you can exhibit passive-aggressive behavior until the moon turns green, but if you do not want to grow and learn, you will not grow and learn. The effort you put into developing your *self* to be the fulfilled, happy person and educator that you deserve to be is up to you. No one can do it for you. The time you spend in quiet, focused introspection can be the most important time you spend in your life. Although some may say they do not have time to sit around delving into what would bring them the greatest joy, I disagree. I believe with all my heart that this can be the most productive time you spend developing yourself and finding peace and fulfillment. To be the person and teacher leader you want to be, you must spend time on in-depth personal assessment, find time for quiet and solitude as well as exercise and recreation, and make an effort to read, research, and identify specific plans to help you grow to be everything you deserve and want to become.

IT'S UP TO YOU

1. How could the quality of teacher leadership enhancement be evaluated?

2. What standards for teacher enhancement would you recommend using for assessment purposes? Why? Support your responses.

3. Explain why leadership development is an important personal and educational goal.

4. Does personal and educational goal attainment depend on a better understanding of leadership itself? If so, how can this be achieved?

5. Which is more important: evaluation of the nature of leadership or the actual development of teachers themselves? Why?

6. Develop an ideal plan for teacher leadership enhancement in a public or private school.

A teacher leader can enhance systematic school improvement by . . .

- Making time for solitude, self-reflection, soul searching, and activities or hobbies that help you relax and bring you peace and enjoyment
- Actively participating in growth activities such as book studies, peer classroom observations, formal staff development sessions, professional conferences, university study, and online courses
- Volunteering to serve as the leader for campus and district committees such as curriculum committees, site-based decision making, wellness activities, surveys, Saturday school, and other activities
- Facilitating the development and implementation of wellness and other campus physical and emotional well-being activities
- Collaborating with campus administrators to develop focus groups to determine what barriers keep teachers from feeling appropriately empowered and to encourage and facilitate positive change for school and classroom improvement
- Facilitating the development and implementation of a need assessment to determine what topics teachers would like to receive additional training in
- Brainstorming creative ways to implement staff suggestions into campus staff development offerings
- Taking an active role in the mentoring of new or struggling teachers, which has been shown to have positive effects for both the mentor and the person being mentored

- Soliciting guest speakers for faculty meetings who are known specialists in areas of campus needs
- Actively participating in annual planning workshops and school board meetings
- Continually encouraging change in areas that need improvement
- Sharing successful ideas with others
- Participating in lifelong learning opportunities inside and outside the field of education
- Remembering that a school's effectiveness is enhanced by the increased autonomy of its teachers
- Consistently encouraging other teachers to also become teacher leaders

Bringing It All Together

"Live the life you have imagined."

—Henry Thoreau

We have come so far in our journey toward teacher leadership. We have discussed what teacher leaders are and why they are so critical to the success of our schools and society today and tomorrow. We have talked about the important role of having a school and classroom vision of success. Vision is not where we are today. It is where we want to be in the future. What knowledge, skills, and attitudes do we want students who leave our schools and classrooms to have and display? What are the resources we need to get us from where we are, which is our current reality, to where we want to be, which is our vision of the way we want our students and classrooms to become? In order to achieve the vision, we must work collaboratively to empower and incorporate the entire school community. Together we must develop, articulate, implement, and be good stewards of the vision to ensure that it is achieved. This not only will enhance learning today but also will be our lasting legacy in an improved and increasingly global society.

In order to achieve the vision, we must have teacher leaders who know what their core values and moral codes are, who are willing to spend time in deep reflection, searching their souls to truly identify what is of lasting value to them as educators and as citizens. To pursue the goal of becoming teacher leaders, we must be willing to make changes in our lives, actions, and attitudes to be the people and professionals that we want to become. We must be willing to step back and try to look at ourselves as others see us rather than simply as we see ourselves. Often there are surprising but quite worthy results. To be significant teacher leaders, we must have an intrinsic code of ethics, live our entire lives with integrity, treat all people with fairness, and consistently display a professional demeanor.

Teacher leaders work hard to cultivate a campus and classroom culture and climate that value and set exceedingly high standards and expectations for all students, faculty, and other members of the school community. A teacher leader is committed to creating an ethos of appreciation for everyone and everything that helps students learn. This creates a nurturing and sustaining environment that will hold up even during the most difficult and stressful times that eventually happen to all of us. Teacher leaders thrive on creating and displaying trust and respect for everyone they encounter, whether the person is a 7-year-old second grader or that child's 70-year-old guardian. Finally, teacher leaders are creative people who are constantly seeking to brainstorm new ideas that are innovative and often involve risks. They do all of this based on research and best practices for the purpose of improving student learning and for the subsequent positive impact it will have on human lives, families, and society as a whole.

The curriculum and instruction used by teacher leaders focus on the whole child and seek to meet his or her needs on several levels. This includes academic needs, of course, but goes beyond that to the physical and psychological needs of learners. Teacher leaders remember that it is not their job to do everything for every student but to facilitate the removal of barriers to success so that each student has a meaningful opportunity for success. To achieve this lofty goal, teacher leaders use an engaging and relevant curriculum that means something to students. They use developmentally appropriate instructional strategies. They are continuously watching and assessing to make sure every student is making progress in the learning journey. When they see a student who is not making progress, they do not give up. They realize that the systematic, ongoing assessment they do with their students is a form of research that they cherish as critical to making a difference in the lives of students, families, and the school community. Therefore, they keep trying to get to the bottom of the problem, the causal agent. Then they work with others in the school and school community to resolve these problems and provide all students with the tools they need to learn and grow as productive citizens.

Teacher leaders are undaunted by the changing face of society. They believe in reaching every child regardless of intellectual level, culture, race, or handicap. Teacher leaders are committed to individualizing and respecting individual differences. They seek to mediate and lead efforts toward conflict resolution. They work hard to identify the common ground between widely divergent perspectives and encourage each group to respect, if not agree with, the other. They appreciate that not all students learn in the same way and that society is different now than it was even a single generation ago. They do not live in the past, wishing things were the way they used to be. Rather, they consistently look to the future for the way the world can be. They are idealists who seek to empower others to work together to reach a vision of learning excellence, respect, freedom, and democracy in an increasingly global society.

Teacher leaders know that it doesn't matter nearly as much what you say as how you say it. The same words or phrases can have vastly different meaning and impact depending on how they are said. Teacher leaders need to have both verbal and nonverbal communication skills and understand the nuances and wonderful power of language. Teacher leaders know that to be successful they must learn to listen first before trying to speak. As Covey (1990) said, they realize the importance of seeking first to understand. They accomplish this by being attentive listeners. Rather than focusing on what they are going to say next, they listen intently to not just what the person is saying but why she or he is saying it and what its relevance is. Active listeners seek to get to the cause of conflict before trying to solve it.

Finally, teacher leaders respect the rights of others in the school community and beyond to know what is going on in the school and why. They respect the media, both when things are going well and being reported accordingly and when problems occur and the media seem to be playing it up in a disproportionate way. They go out of their way to communicate their campus and classroom vision to anyone who will listen. They realize that a lack of correct knowledge can lead to wrong perceptions and conflict and that it takes more time and effort to correct misconceptions than it does to be forthcoming in the first place.

Teacher leaders realize the importance of being lifelong learners. They realize that having a degree and certification is only the beginning. They believe Socrates was right when he taught that truth lies within us, so they spend a lot of time looking inward for important answers. They search their hearts and souls to find their strengths and weaknesses and always ask themselves how they can enhance each facet of their lives. "How can I make it better?" is their favorite question, with "it" as a roaming variable for anything in their lives that needs to be improved. Teacher leaders realize the importance of both quiet times and exercise in their lives. They know it is important to find a balance between their personal and professional lives and their cognitive, physical, and psychological

Figure 9.1   Concentric Circles of Success

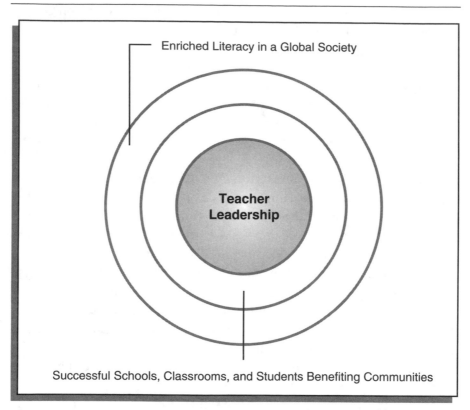

well-being. They know that to continue to grow as both people and experts they must read, research, and participate in professional activities.

The rest is up to you. Figure 9.1 shows the impact teacher leaders can have on creating successful schools, classrooms, and students. Together, these affect both individual communities and the greater global society. Reading this may make you think that the combination of all these factors is just too much effort, that all you really want to do is teach students and go home. Many people are satisfied to do exactly that.

But there are others who want much, much more. They are the teacher leaders of today and the teachers who want to be leaders tomorrow. They have no desire to become principals. They want to be expert educators in their own classrooms, to be footsoldiers in the war on illiteracy, to be true leaders in the learning journey. They want to change the world, one classroom at a time.

I hope this book has been of value in your life as a teacher leader and in your personal life as a citizen and family member. If it has, recommend it to a friend. I encourage you in your steadfast efforts to do everything you can to improve the life of every student. I commend you for the heart and compassion you have shown just by reading this book. I leave you with one parting thought: Go forth, do well, and change the world. After all, if we as teacher leaders do not do it, who will?

IT'S UP TO YOU

1. Define and explain teacher leadership.

2. Why is teacher leadership important in a changing, global society?

3. Describe the role of teacher leaders in increasing learning capacity in classrooms, schools, and communities. Provide realistic examples.

4. Are teacher leadership standards necessary, and, if so, by whom should they be developed, validated, applied, and assessed?

5. Create a set of teacher leadership standards that you think are most important for all educators to have and be measured by.

6. Identify and create a list of goals to improve your effectiveness as a classroom, campus, and community citizen leader. Use a timeline for success and identify specific assessment strategies to guarantee accountability in meeting your goals in a timely manner.

Recommended Reading to Enhance Teacher Leadership

Vision

If we don't know where we want to be as teacher leaders, how will we know when we get there?

Batey, C. S. (1996). *Parents are lifesavers: A handbook for parent involvement in schools.* Thousand Oaks, CA: Corwin Press.

Bennis, W. (1989). *Why leaders can't lead.* San Francisco: Jossey-Bass.

Bennis, W. (1999). *Old dogs, new tricks.* Provo, UT: Executive Excellence.

Blanchard, K., & Bowles, S. (1998). *Gung-ho!* New York: William Morrow.

Bolman, L. G., & Deal, T. E. (1997). *Reframing organizations: Artistry, choice, and leadership* (2nd ed.). San Francisco: Jossey-Bass.

Bolman, L. G., & Deal, T. E. (2001). *Leading with soul: An uncommon journey of spirit.* San Francisco: Jossey-Bass.

Brock, B. L., & Grady, M. L. (2000). *Rekindling the flame: Principals combating teacher burnout.* Thousand Oaks, CA: Corwin Press.

Covey, S. R., Merrill, A. R., & Merrill, R. R. (1994). *First things first.* New York: Simon & Schuster.

Deal, T. E., & Bolman, L. G. (2001). *Leading with soul.* San Francisco: Jossey-Bass.

Deal, T. E., & Peterson, K. D. (1994). *The leadership paradox.* San Francisco: Jossey-Bass.

Deal, T., & Peterson, K. (1999). *Shaping school culture: The heart of leadership.* San Francisco: Jossey-Bass.

De Pree, M. (1989). *Leadership is an art.* New York: Dell.

De Pree, M. (1997). *Leading without power: Finding hope in serving community.* San Francisco: Jossey-Bass.

Dickmann, M. H., & Stanford-Blair, N. (2001). *Connecting leadership to the brain.* Thousand Oaks, CA: Corwin Press.

Drucker, F. (1996). *The leader of the future.* San Francisco: Jossey-Bass.

Elias, M. J., Arnold, H., & Hussey, C. S. (Eds.). (2002). *EQ + IQ = best leadership practices for caring and successful schools.* Thousand Oaks, CA: Corwin Press.

English, F. W. (1994). *Theory in educational administration.* New York: HarperCollins.

Erlandson, D. A., Stark, P. L., & Ward, S. M. (1996). *Organizational oversight: Planning and scheduling for effectiveness.* Larchmont, NY: Eye on Education.

Fitzwater, I. (1996). *Time management for school administrators.* Rockport, MA: Pro>Active Publications.

Glanz, J. (1998). *Action research: An educational guide to school improvement.* Norwood, MA: Christopher Gordan.

Holcomb, E. L. (2004). *Getting excited about data: Combining people, passion, and proof to maximize student achievement* (2nd ed.). Thousand Oaks, CA: Corwin Press.

Hoy, W. H., & Miskel, C. G. (1996). *Educational administration: Theory, research, and practice* (5th ed.). New York: McGraw-Hill.

Hoyle, J. (2001). *Leadership and the force of love: Six keys to motivating with love.* Thousand Oaks, CA: Corwin Press.

Hoyle, J. R. (2006). *Leadership and futuring: Making visions happen* (2nd ed.). Thousand Oaks, CA: Corwin Press.

Johnson, S., & Blanchard, K. (Eds.). (1998). *Who moved my cheese? An amazing way to deal with change in your work and in your life.* New York: G. P. Putnam's Sons.

Ledeen, M. A. (1999). *Machiavelli on modern leadership.* New York: St. Martin's Press.

MacKay, L. L., & Ralston, E. W. (1998). *Creating better schools: What authentic principals do.* Thousand Oaks, CA: Corwin Press.

Murphy, J. F., & Datnow, A. (2002). *Leadership lessons from comprehensive school reforms.* Thousand Oaks, CA: Corwin Press.

Odden, A. R., & Archibald, S. J. (2000). *Reallocating resources: How to boost student achievement without asking for more.* Thousand Oaks, CA: Corwin Press.

Palestini, R. H. (1999). *Educational administration: Leading with mind and heart.* Lancaster, PA: Technomic Publishing.

Pellicer, L. O. (2003). *Caring enough to lead: How reflective thought leads to moral leadership* (2nd ed.). Thousand Oaks, CA: Corwin Press.

Peterson, K. D. (2002). *Effective teacher hiring: A guide to getting the best.* Alexandria, VA: Association for Supervision & Curriculum Development.

Ramsey, R. D. (2000). *Fiscal fitness for school administrators: How to stretch resources and do even more with less.* Thousand Oaks, CA: Corwin Press.

Ramsey, R. D. (2005). *Lead, follow, or get out of the way: How to be a more effective leader in today's schools* (2nd ed.). Thousand Oaks, CA: Corwin Press.

Schlechty, P. C. (2001). *Shaking up the school house.* San Francisco: Jossey-Bass.

Sergiovanni, T. J. (2000). *The lifeworld of leadership.* San Francisco: Jossey-Bass.

Sergiovanni, T. J., & Starratt, R. J. (1998). *Supervision: A redefinition* (6th ed.). Boston: McGraw-Hill.

Snowden, P. E., & Gorton, R. A. (1998). *School leadership and administration: Important concepts, case studies, and simulations* (5th ed.). New York: McGraw-Hill.

Spears, L., Lawrence, M., & Blanchard, K. (2002). *Focus on leadership: Servant-leadership for the 21st century.* New York: John Wiley & Sons.

Ethics and Integrity

Just because something is legal does not necessarily mean it is the right thing for teachers as leaders to do.

Blanchard, K., & Peale, N. V. (1988). *The power of ethical management.* New York: Fawcett Columbine.

DiGiulio, R. C. (2001). *Educate, medicate, or litigate? What teachers, parents, and administrators must do about student behavior.* Thousand Oaks, CA: Corwin Press.

Doyle, D. P., & Pimentel, S. (1999). *Raising the standard: An eight-step action guide for schools and communities* (2nd ed.). Thousand Oaks, CA: Corwin Press.

Fiore, D. J., & Whitaker, T. (2001). *Dealing with difficult parents (and with parents in difficult situations).* Larchmont, NY: Eye on Education.

Josephson, M. S., & Hanson, W. (1998). *The power of character.* San Francisco: Jossey-Bass.

Kosmoski, G. J., & Pollack, D. R. (2005). *Managing difficult, frustrating, and hostile conversations: Strategies for savvy administrators* (2nd ed.). Thousand Oaks, CA: Corwin Press.

McEwan, E. K. (1996). *Leading your team to excellence: How to make quality decisions.* Thousand Oaks, CA: Corwin Press.

McEwan, E. K. (2004). *How to deal with parents who are angry, troubled, afraid, or just plain crazy* (2nd ed.). Thousand Oaks, CA: Corwin Press.

Osier, J. L., & Fox, H. P. (2001). *Settle conflicts right now! A step-by-step guide for K–6 classrooms.* Thousand Oaks, CA: Corwin Press.

Podesta, C. (2001). *Self-esteem and the 6-second secret* (updated ed.). Thousand Oaks, CA: Corwin Press.

Podesta, C., & Sanderson, V. (1999). *Life would be easy if it weren't for other people.* Thousand Oaks, CA: Corwin Press.

Seiler, T. L. (2001). *Developing your case for support.* San Francisco: Jossey-Bass.

Sergiovanni, T. J. (1992). *Moral leadership: Getting to the heart of school improvement.* San Francisco: Jossey-Bass.

Sperry, D. J. (1999). *Working in a legal and regulatory environment: A handbook for school leaders.* Larchmont, NY: Eye on Education.

Streshly, W. A., Walsh, J., & Frase, L. E. (2001). *Avoiding legal hassles: What school administrators really need to know* (2nd ed.). Thousand Oaks, CA: Corwin Press.

Thomas, O., & Haynes, C. C. (2001). *Finding common ground: A guide to religious liberty in public schools.* Nashville, TN: First Amendment Center.

Van Geel, T., & Imber, M. (2000). *Education law* (2nd ed.). Mahwah, NJ: Lawrence Erlbaum.

Whitaker, T. (1999). *Dealing with difficult teachers.* Larchmont, NY: Eye on Education.

Curriculum and Instruction

Curriculum is what we teach. Instruction is how we teach it. Together they are the meat and potatoes of what education and teacher leadership are all about.

Arter, J., & McTighe, J. (2000). *Scoring rubrics in the classroom: Using performance criteria for assessing and improving student performance.* Thousand Oaks, CA: Corwin Press.

Beach, D. M., & Reinhartz, J. (2000). *Supervisory leadership.* Boston: Allyn & Bacon.

Beane, J. A. (1997). *Curriculum integration: Designing the core of democratic education.* New York: Teachers College Press.

Bracey, G. W. (2000). *Bail me out! Handling difficult data and tough questions about public schools.* Thousand Oaks, CA: Corwin Press.

Carbo, M. (2000). *What every principal should know about teaching reading.* Syosset, NY: National Reading Styles Institute.

Costa, A. L., & Garmston, R. J. (1994). *Cognitive coaching.* Norwood, MA: Christopher Gordon.

Creighton, T. B. (2006). *Schools and data: The educator's guide for using data to improve decision making* (2nd ed.). Thousand Oaks, CA: Corwin Press.

English, F. W. (1999). *Deciding what to teach and test: Developing, aligning, and auditing the curriculum* (millennium ed.). Thousand Oaks, CA: Corwin Press.

Erickson, H. L. (2002). *Concept-based curriculum and instruction: Teaching beyond the facts.* Thousand Oaks, CA: Corwin Press.

Glenn, H. S., & Brock, M. L. (1998). *7 strategies for developing capable students.* Roseville, CA: Prima Publishing.

Gregory, G. H., & Chapman, C. (2006). *Differentiated instructional strategies: One size doesn't fit all* (2nd ed.). Thousand Oaks, CA: Corwin Press.

Hadaway, N., Vardell, S. M., & Young, T. (2001). *Literature-based instruction with English language learners.* Boston: Allyn & Bacon.

Harris, S. (2005). *Bravo teacher!: Building relationships with actions that value others.* Larchmont, NY: Eye on Education.

Hoyle, J. H., English, F., & Steffy, B. (1998). *Skills for successful 21st century school leaders.* Arlington, VA: American Association of School Administrators.

Kaser, J. S., Mundry, S. E., Stiles, K. E., & Loucks-Horsley, S. (2006). *Leading every day: 124 actions for effective leadership* (2nd ed.). Thousand Oaks, CA: Corwin Press.

Leithwood, K. A., Aitken, R., & Jantzi, D. (2006). *Making schools smarter: Leading with evidence* (3rd ed.). Thousand Oaks, CA: Corwin Press.

Lunenburg, F. C., & Ornstein, A. C. (2000). *Educational administration: Concepts and practices* (3rd ed.). Belmont, CA: Wadsworth/Thomas Learning.

Marlowe, B. A., & Page, M. L. (2005). *Creating and sustaining the constructivist classroom* (2nd ed.). Thousand Oaks, CA: Corwin Press.

Oliva, P. F. (1997). *Supervision in today's schools* (5th ed.). New York: John Wiley & Sons.

Parsons, B. A. (2001). *Evaluative inquiry: Using evaluation to promote student success.* Thousand Oaks, CA: Corwin Press.

Pratt, D. (1994). *Curriculum planning: A handbook for professionals.* Ft. Worth, TX: Harcourt Brace College.

Reinhartz, J., & Beach, D. M. (2001). *Foundations of educational leadership: Changing schools, changing roles.* Boston: Allyn & Bacon.

Reksten, L. E. (2000). *Using technology to increase student learning.* Thousand Oaks, CA: Corwin Press.

Schroth, G., Berkeley, T. R., & Fishbaugh, M. S. (2002). *Ensuring safe school environments.* Mahwah, NJ: Lawrence Erlbaum.

Sharp, W. L., Walter, J. K., & Sharp, H. M. (1998). *Case studies for school leaders: Implementing the ISLLC standards.* Lancaster, PA: Technomic Publishing.

Solomon, P. G. (2002). *The assessment bridge: Positive ways to link tests to learning, standards, and curriculum improvement.* Thousand Oaks, CA: Corwin Press.

Thomas, S. J. (1999). *Designing surveys that work! A step-by-step guide.* Thousand Oaks, CA: Corwin Press.

Thompson, S. J., Quenemoen, R. F., Thurlow, M. L., & Ysseldyke, J. E. (2001). *Alternate assessments for students with disabilities.* Thousand Oaks, CA: Corwin Press.

Thurlow, M. L., Elliott, J. L., & Ysseldyke, J. E. (2002). *Testing students with disabilities: Practical strategies for complying with district and state requirements* (2nd ed.). Thousand Oaks, CA: Corwin Press.

Trump, K. S. (1997). *Practical school security: Basic guidelines for safe and secure schools.* Thousand Oaks, CA: Corwin Press.

Veale, J. R., Morley, R. E., & Erickson, C. L. (2001). *Practical evaluation for collaborative services: Goals, processes, tools, and reporting systems for school-based programs.* Thousand Oaks, CA: Corwin Press.

Wachter, J. C. (1999). *Classroom volunteers: Uh-oh! or right on!* Thousand Oaks, CA: Corwin Press.

Worthen, B., Sanders, J., & Fitzpatrick, J. (1996). *Program evaluation, alternative approaches and practical guidelines* (2nd ed.). New York: Addison-Wesley.

Equity for All Learners

Just because an instructional strategy has worked in the past does not necessarily mean it is appropriate for all learners in today's increasingly diverse society. We must meet the challenge of addressing the needs of every student.

Banks, J. A., & Banks, C. M. (1996). *Multicultural education: Issues and perspectives.* Boston: Allyn & Bacon.

Burrello, L. C., Lashley, C., & Beatty, E. E. (2000). *Educating all students together: How school leaders create unified systems.* Thousand Oaks, CA: Corwin Press.

Fullan, M. (2001). *Leading in a culture of change.* San Francisco: Jossey-Bass.

Henze, R., Katz, A., Norte, E., Sather, S. E., & Walker, E. (2002). *Leading for diversity: How school leaders promote positive interethnic relations.* Thousand Oaks, CA: Corwin Press.

Kozol, J. (1992). *Savage inequalities: Children in America's schools.* New York: Harper Perennial Library.

Kozol, J. (2000). *Ordinary resurrections: Children in the years of hope.* New York: Crown.

Nielsen, L. B. (2002). *Brief reference of student disabilities with strategies for the classroom.* Thousand Oaks, CA: Corwin Press.

Obiakor, F. E., & Ford, B. A. (2002). *Creating successful learning environments for African American learners with exceptionalities.* Thousand Oaks, CA: Corwin Press.

Payne, R. K. (1998). *A framework for understanding poverty.* Baytown, TX: RFT Publishing.

Slavin, R. E., & Fashola, O. S. (1998). *Show me the evidence! Proven and promising programs for America's schools.* Thousand Oaks, CA: Corwin Press.

Tomlinson, C. A. (1999). *The differentiated classroom: Responding to the needs of all learners.* Alexandria, VA: Association for Supervision & Curriculum Development.

Tomlinson, C. A. (2001). *How to differentiate instruction in mixed-ability classrooms* (2nd ed.). Alexandria, VA: Association for Supervision & Curriculum Development.

Tomlinson, C. A., & Allan, S. D. (2000). *Leadership for differentiating schools and classrooms.* Alexandria, VA: Association for Supervision & Curriculum Development.

Woodward, J., & Cuban, L. (Eds.). (2000). *Technology, curriculum, and professional development: Adapting schools to meet the needs of students with disabilities.* Thousand Oaks, CA: Corwin Press.

Communication Skills

> We can be the smartest people ever to have lived, but if we can't communicate effectively and motivate our students, then our vast intelligence or abundant academic knowledge does not mean a thing.

Barker, C. L., & Searchwell, C. J. (2000). *Writing year-end teacher improvement plans—right now!! The principal's time-saving reference guide.* Thousand Oaks, CA: Corwin Press.

Barker, C. L., & Searchwell, C. J. (2003). *Writing meaningful teacher evaluations—right now!! The principal's quick-start reference guide* (2nd ed.). Thousand Oaks, CA: Corwin Press.

benShea, N. (2000). *What every principal would like to say . . . and what to say next time.* Thousand Oaks, CA: Corwin Press.

Brewer, E. W., DeJonge, J. O., & Stout, V. J. (2001). *Moving online: Making the transition from traditional instruction and communication strategies.* Thousand Oaks, CA: Corwin Press.

Decker, R. H. (1997). *When a crisis hits: Will your school be ready?* Thousand Oaks, CA: Corwin Press.

Epstein, J. L., Sanders, M. G., Simon, B. S., Salinas, K. C., Jansorn, N. R., & Van Voorhis, F. L. (2002). *School, family, and community partnerships: Your handbook for action* (2nd ed.). Thousand Oaks, CA: Corwin Press.

Holcomb, E. L. (2000). *Asking the right questions: Techniques for collaboration and school change* (2nd ed.). Thousand Oaks, CA: Corwin Press.

Jayanthi, M., & Nelson, J. S. (2001). *Savvy decision making: An administrator's guide to using focus groups in schools.* Thousand Oaks, CA: Corwin Press.

Kouzes, J. M., & Posner, B. Z. (1998). *Encouraging the heart: A leader's guide to rewarding and recognizing others.* San Francisco: Jossey-Bass.

Peterson, S. (2000). *The grantwriter's Internet companion: A resource for educators and others seeking grants and funding.* Thousand Oaks, CA: Corwin Press.

Whitaker, T. A., Whitaker, B., & Lumpa, D. (2000). *Motivating & inspiring teachers: The educational leader's guide for building staff morale.* Larchmont, NY: Eye on Education.

Teacher Enhancement

> If we are not growing, we are standing still while the world surges ahead. The gap between our knowledge, skills, and dispositions and the ever-changing needs of students continues to widen. Consequently, by standing still we are moving backwards. Leaders do not move backwards. They march forward. How can we as teachers march forward to improve ourselves as educators and human beings for now and the future?

Anderson, J. W. (2000). *The answers to questions that teachers most frequently ask.* Thousand Oaks, CA: Corwin Press.

Ardovino, J., Hollingsworth, J., & Ybarra, S. (2000). *Multiple measures: Accurate ways to assess student achievement.* Thousand Oaks, CA: Corwin Press.

Bennis, W. (1997). *Managing people is like herding cats.* Provo, UT: Executive Excellence.

Bigge, M. L., & Shermis, S. S. (1999). *Learning theories for teachers* (6th ed.). New York: Addison-Wesley Longman.

Blanchard, K., Hybels, B., & Hodges, P. (1999). *Leadership by the book: Tools to transform your workplace.* New York: William Morrow.

Blanchard, K., & Johnson, S. (1981). *The one minute manager.* New York: Berkley.

Blanchard, K. H., Oncken, W., Jr., & Burrows, H. (1989). *The one minute manager meets the monkey.* New York: William Morrow.

Blanchard, K., Zigarmi, P., & Zigarmi, D. (1985). *Leadership and the one minute manager.* New York: William Morrow.

Blase, J., & Kirby, P. C. (1999). *Bringing out the best in teachers: What effective principals do* (2nd ed.). Thousand Oaks, CA: Corwin Press.

Brewer, E. W., Achilles, C. M., Fuhriman, J. R., & Hollingsworth, C. (2001). *Finding funding: Grantwriting from start to finish, including project management and Internet use* (4th ed.). Thousand Oaks, CA: Corwin Press.

Brock, B. L., & Grady, M. L. (2001). *From first-year to first-rate: Principals guiding beginning teachers* (2nd ed.). Thousand Oaks, CA: Corwin Press.

Burke, M. A., & Picus, L. O. (2001). *Developing community-empowered schools.* Thousand Oaks, CA: Corwin Press.

Coleman, M., & Anderson, L. (2001). *Managing finance and resources in education.* Thousand Oaks, CA: Corwin Press.

Covey, S. R. (1990). *Principle-centered leadership.* New York: Simon & Schuster.

Danielson, C., & McGreal, T. L. (2000). *Teacher evaluation to enhance professional practice.* Princeton, NJ: Educational Testing Service.

Daresh, J. C. (2001). *Leaders helping leaders: A practical guide to administrative mentoring* (2nd ed.). Thousand Oaks, CA: Corwin Press.

Daresh, J. C. (2002). *Teachers mentoring teachers: A practical approach to helping new and experienced staff.* Thousand Oaks, CA: Corwin Press.

Denmark, V. M., & Podsen, I. J. (2000). *Coaching and mentoring first-year and student teachers.* Larchmont, NY: Eye on Education.

DeWitt Wallace–Reader's Digest Fund Study Conference. (1992). *Developing a framework for the continual professional development of administrators in the Northeast.* (ERIC Document Reproduction Service No. ED383104)

Gray, K. C. (1999). *Getting real: Helping teens find their future.* Thousand Oaks, CA: Corwin Press.

Irby, B. J., & Brown, G. (2000). *The career advancement portfolio.* Thousand Oaks, CA: Corwin Press.

Joyce, B., & Weil, M. (1996). *Models of teaching.* Needham Heights, MA: Simon & Schuster.

Krzyzewski, M., & Phillips, D. T. (2000). *Leading with the heart: Coach K's successful strategies for basketball, business, and life.* New York: Warner Business Books.

Maxwell, J. C. (1995). *Developing the leaders around you.* Nashville, TN: Thomas Nelson.

McNamara, J. F., Erlandson, D. A., & McNamara, M. (1999). *Measurement and evaluation: Strategies for school improvement.* Larchmont, NY: Eye on Education.

Peters, T., & Waterman, R. H. (1993). *In search of excellence.* New York: Warner Books.

Podsen, I. J. (2002). *Teacher retention: What is your weakest link?* Larchmont, NY: Eye on Education.

Sanders, J. R., & Sullins, C. D. (2005). *Evaluating school programs: An educator's guide* (3rd ed.). Thousand Oaks, CA: Corwin Press.

Showers, B., & Joyce, B. (2002). *Student achievement through staff development* (3rd ed.). Alexandria, VA: Association for Supervision & Curriculum Development.

Smith, H. W. (1994). *The 10 natural laws of successful time and life management.* New York: Warner.

Weil, J., Weil, B., & Weil, M. (1998). *Models of teaching* (6th ed.). Needham Heights, MA: Simon & Schuster.

Wolfe, P. (2001). *Brain matters. Translating research into classroom practice.* Alexandria, VA: Association for Supervision & Curriculum Development.

Wyatt, R. L., III, & Looper, S. (2003). *So you have to have a portfolio: A teacher's guide to preparation and presentation* (2nd ed.). Thousand Oaks, CA: Corwin Press.

York-Barr, J., Sommers, W. A., Ghere, G. S., & Montie, J. (2005). *Reflective practice to improve schools: An action guide for educators* (2nd ed.). Thousand Oaks, CA: Corwin Press.

References

Ackerman, R., & Mackenzie, S. (2006). Uncovering teacher leadership. *Educational Leadership, 63*(8), 66–70. Retrieved September 6, 2006, from the Professional Development Collection database.

Agnes, M. (Ed.). (2001). *Webster's new world college dictionary* (4th ed.). Foster City, CA: IDG Books Worldwide.

Barth, R. (1991). *Improving schools from within: Teachers, parents, and principals can make the difference.* San Francisco: Jossey-Bass.

Beaudoin, M.-N., & Taylor, M. E. (2004). *Creating a positive school culture: How principals and teachers can solve problems together.* Thousand Oaks, CA: Corwin Press.

Bennis, W. (1989). *On becoming a leader.* New York: Basic Books.

Blair, J. (2003). With support, teachers would stay put, report finds. *Education Week, 22*(21), 5. Retrieved September 5, 2006, from the Professional Development Collection database.

Collins, J. (2001). *Good to great.* New York: HarperCollins.

Covey, S. R. (1990). *The 7 habits of highly effective people.* New York: Simon & Schuster.

Danielson, C. (2006). *Teacher leadership that strengthens professional practice.* Alexandria, VA: Association for Supervision & Curriculum Development.

Fullan, M. (2001). *The new meaning of educational change.* New York: Teachers College Press.

Glaser, J. P. (2004). *Leading through collaboration: Guiding groups to productive solutions.* Thousand Oaks, CA: Corwin Press.

Greenleaf, R. (1982). *Servant as leader.* Westfield, IN: Robert Greenleaf Center.

Greenleaf, R. K. (1991). *Servant leadership: A journey into the nature of legitimate power and greatness.* New York: Paulist Press.

Harris, S. (2005). *Bravo teacher!: Building relationships with actions that value others.* Larchmont, NY: Eye on Education.

Hook, D. P. (2006). *The impact of teacher leadership on school effectiveness in selected exemplary secondary schools.* Unpublished doctoral dissertation, Texas A&M University, College Station.

Hoyle, J. R. (2001). *Leadership and the force of love: Six keys to motivating with love.* Thousand Oaks, CA: Corwin Press.

Krisko, M. E. (2001). *Teacher leadership: A profile to identify the potential.* (Report No. SP040365). Paper presented at the Biennial Convocation of Kappa Delta Pi, Orlando, FL. (ERIC Document Reproduction Service No. ED459147)

Little, J. (1985). *Cases in emerging leadership by teachers: The school-level instructional support team.* San Francisco: Far West Laboratory for Educational Research and Development.

Moller, G., & Pankake, A. (2006). *Lead with me: A principal's guide to teacher leadership.* Larchmont, NY: Eye on Education.

Murphy, J. F. (2005). *Connecting teacher leadership and school improvement.* Thousand Oaks, CA: Corwin Press.

Murphy, J. F., Beck, L. G., Crawford, M. W., Hodges, A., & McGaughy, C. L. (2001). *The productive high school: Creating personalized academic communities.* Thousand Oaks, CA: Corwin Press.

N.C. University, colleges team up to fight teacher shortage. (2004). *Community College Week, 16*(17), 14–16. Retrieved September 5, 2006, from the Professional Development Collection database.

Ng, J. (2003). Teacher shortages in urban schools. *Education & Urban Society, 35*(4), 380. Retrieved September 5, 2006, from the Professional Development Collection database.

Overholser, J. (1992). Socrates in the classroom. *College Teaching, 40*(1), 14–20.

Palincsar, A. S., & Brown, A. L. (1984). Reciprocal teaching of comprehension fostering and monitoring strategies. *Cognition and Instruction, 1,* 117–175.

Patrikakou, E., Weissberg, R., Redding, S., & Walberg, H. (Eds.). (2005). *School–family partnerships for children's success.* New York: Teachers College Press.

Pellicer, L. O. (2003). *Caring enough to lead: How reflective thought leads to moral leadership* (2nd ed.). Thousand Oaks, CA: Corwin Press.

Peters, T. (1987). *Thriving on chaos: Handbook for a management revolution.* New York: Random House.

Roberts, S. M., & Pruitt, E. Z. (2003). *Schools as professional learning communities: Collaborative activities and strategies for professional development.* Thousand Oaks, CA: Corwin Press.

Rubin, H. (2002). *Collaborative leadership: Developing effective partnerships in communities and schools.* Thousand Oaks, CA: Corwin Press.

Strodl, P. (1992, March). *A model of teacher leadership.* Paper presented at the annual meeting of the Eastern Educational Research Association, Hilton Head, SC.

Sullivan, S., & Glanz, J. (2005). Building effective learning communities: *Strategies for leadership, learning, & collaboration.* Thousand Oaks, CA: Corwin Press.

Suranna, K. J. (2000). *The nature of teacher leadership: A case study of elementary school teachers from a five-year teacher education program.* Unpublished doctoral dissertation, University of Connecticut, Storrs.

Suranna, K. J., & Moss, D. M. (1999). *Describing preservice teachers' conceptions of the role of teacher leader.* Paper presented at the annual meeting of the Educational Research Association, Ellenville, NY. (ERIC Document Reproduction Service No. ED447078)

Suranna, K. J., & Moss, D. M. (2002). *Exploring teacher leadership in the context of teacher preparation.* Paper presented at the annual meeting of the Educational Research Association, New Orleans, LA. (ERIC Document Reproduction Service No. ED465751)

Williams, E. (1999). The comfort of strangers. *Times Educational Supplement, 4323,* 14. Retrieved September 5, 2006, from the Professional Development Collection database.

Wilmore, E. (2004). *Principal induction: A standards-based model for administrator development.* Thousand Oaks, CA: Corwin Press.

Index

Ackerman, R., 3, 4
Action planning, 15-16, 15 (figure)
Active listening, 3, 44,
      78-79 (figures), 79-80, 82-83
Administrators, xiii, 1
   active listening and, 44
   learning communities and, 11-12
   shared leadership and, 2, 3
   teacher leaders as threats, 4
   See also Teacher leadership; Vision
Aligned curriculum, 12, 57,
      58 (figure)
Appreciation, 42-43, 45-46
Assessment, 12
   alignment with curriculum,
      57, 58 (figure)
   in-depth personal assessment,
      91-93, 92 (figure),
      100-101, 109-110
   ongoing systematic assessment,
      58-59, 61-62
   school/district performance
      ratings, 67

Barth, R., 4
Belief systems. *See* Equity for
   all learners
Block scheduling, 12

Care ethic, xi, 81
Certification, xiii, 109
Change agents, 2, 3, 17, 54
Citizenship skills, 15
Civil interaction, 68

Classroom context, 1, 3
   ideal-practice discrepancy and,
      3, 44-45, 53-54
   volunteers, 57
   See also Classroom culture/climate;
      Curriculum/instruction;
      Instructional leadership;
      Teacher leadership
Classroom culture/climate, 40-42, 42
      (figure), 49-50, 108
   ethos of expectations/appreciation/
      success and, 42-43, 45-46
   innovation and, 44-45, 48-49
   organizational culture/climate
      example, 39-41
   philosophical framework for, 42-45
   positive feedback and, 3, 42
   problem-based learning and, 45-49
   respect/mutual trust and,
      43-44, 46-48
   systematic school improvement
      and, 50-51
   See also Classroom context; Equity
      for all learners; Student
      performance
Collaborative leadership, 3, 4, 11
   common vision of excellence and,
      69, 70 (figure), 73-74
   learning communities and, 12
   vision, development of, 13-16,
      13 (figure), 15 (figure), 22
Collins, J., 90
Common ground, 67-68, 67 (figure),
      70-71, 109

Common vision of excellence, 69, 70 (figure), 73-74
Communication skills, 5, 6, 11, 77-78, 86, 109
  active/effective listening, 78-79 (figure), 79-80, 82-83
  interpreters and, 82
  language, power of, 80-81, 83-84
  philosophical framework for, 78-82
  problem-based learning and, 82-86
  public's right to know, 81-82, 81 (figure), 84-86, 109
  resource materials for, 118
  systematic school improvement and, 87
  verbal/nonverbal communication, 109
  vision and, 12-13, 16, 19-20
Communities. See Learning communities
Conferences, 3, 56, 57, 99
Conflict resolution, 109
Consensus building models, 14
Continuous enhancement, 91, 98-100, 99 (figure), 103-104
Cooperative learning, 57
Core concepts, xiv, 4-5
Core values. See Ethics/integrity
Covey, S. R., 11, 79, 109
Creative teaching, 3
Critical thinking, 5, 14, 16
Culture. See Classroom culture/climate
Curriculum/instruction, 3, 4, 6, 53-55, 62-63, 108
  alignment with assessment, 12, 57, 58 (figure)
  assessment data and, 53
  developmentally appropriate instruction, 57, 60-61
  differentiated instruction, 64
  engaging/relevant curriculum, 55-56, 59-60
  improved student performance, elements of, 55, 56 (figure)
  individual learning styles and, 53

ongoing systematic assessment, 58-59, 61-62
  philosophical framework for, 55-59
  problem-based learning and, 59-62
  professional development opportunities and, 56
  resource materials for, 115-117
  systematic school improvement and, 64
  See also Classroom context; Equity for all learners; Instructional leadership

Data-driven decisions, 14-15
Decision making:
  data-driven decision making, 14-15
  learning communities and, 12
  teacher participation in, 2
Developmentally appropriate instruction, 56 (figure), 57, 60-61
Differences. See Equity for all learners
Differentiated instruction, 64, 65-66, 66 (figure), 69
Direct instructional approach, 4
Diversity. See Equity for all learners
Dropouts, 18-19

Effective listening, 78-79 (figure), 79-80, 82-83
Empowerment, 2, 12, 109
Engaging curriculum, 55-56, 56 (figure), 59-60
Enhancement. See Continuous enhancement; Teacher enhancement
Equity for all learners, 5, 12, 13, 74, 108-109
  common ground, identification of/respect for, 67-68, 67 (figure), 70-71
  common vision of excellence, 69, 70 (figure), 73-74

diversity/multiculturalism and,
65-66, 66 (figure)
fairness ethic and, 28-29, 32-34
learning/social differences,
acceptance/appreciation of,
68-69, 71-72
philosophical framework
for, 66-70
problem-based learning and, 70-74
resource materials for, 117
systematic school improvement
and, 75-76
Established core values/moral code,
27-28, 29-31
Ethics/integrity, 4, 5, 25-26,
35-36, 107-108
care ethic, xi, 81
ethics, established core
values/moral code and,
27-28, 29-31
fairness ethic, 28-29, 32-34, 44
group ethic, 2
integrity, personal core
values/moral code and,
28, 31-32
learning/societal differences,
acceptance/appreciation of,
68-69, 70 (figure)
philosophical framework for, 26-29
problem-based learning and, 29-35
professional demeanor and,
29, 34-35
reciprocal determination cycle and,
27 (figure), 28
resource materials for, 114-115
systematic school improvement
and, 37
See also Teacher leadership; Vision
Expectations, xiv, 16, 42 (figure),
42-43, 45-46, 54

Fairness ethic, 28-29, 32-34, 44
Flexibility, 3, 57
Formal teacher leader roles, 3
Fullan, M., 4

Global society, 44, 110, 110 (figure)
Greenleaf, R. K., 4
Group ethic, 2, 11
Group learning activities, 69, 78

Hands-on learning, 57, 69
Harris, S., 4
Hook, D. P., 4
How-can-I-make-it-better model,
93-95, 94 (figure)

Improvement. See Continuous
enhancement; Learning
communities; Systematic school
improvement; Teacher
enhancement; Vision
Independent learners, 69
In-depth personal assessment,
91-93, 92 (figure),
100-101, 109-110
Individualized education plan
(IEP), 44
Inductive reasoning, 5
Informal leadership roles, 2, 3
Innovative approach, 12, 42
(figure), 44-45
Instructional leadership, 2
innovation and, 12, 42 (figure),
44-45
risk taking and, 3, 17, 44
self-discovery process, 4
Socratic approach and, 4-6
stand-and-deliver direct
instruction and, 4
See also Classroom culture/climate;
Curriculum/instruction
Integrity. See Ethics/
integrity
Interstate Council of Chief School
Executives, xiv
Interstate New Teacher
Assessment and
Support Consortium
(INTASC), xiv
Interpersonal/intrapersonal skills, 3

Kinesthetic activities, 57, 69
Krisko, M. E., 3

Language. *See* Communication skills
Leadership development, xiii, xiv
  development from within, 3-4
  servant leadership model and, 4-5
  Socratic method and, 4-6
  See also Learning communities;
    Teacher leadership
Learning communities:
  constituents of, 11-12
  decision process and, 12
  definition of, 11
  growth/learning focus of, 12
  improvement focus of, 11
  vision/mission, communication
    of, 12-13
  See also Administrators;
    Problem-based learning;
    Student performance; Teacher
    leadership; Vision
Learning differences, 68-69,
  71-72, 108-109
Learning disabilities, 65, 66, 69
Learning styles, 69
Lifelong learning, 3, 12, 98, 109
Listening effectively, 78-79 (figures),
  79-80, 82-83
Little, J. W., 4

Mackenzie, S., 3, 4
Meetings, 3, 56
Mentoring, 3, 11, 57, 64
Mission, 12, 16
Modeling behaviors, 3, 64, 78
Moller, G., 4
Moral code. *See* Equity for all
  learners; Ethics/integrity
Moss, D. M., 2, 3
Multiculturalism. *See* Equity for all
  learners
Murphy, J. F., 4
Mutual trust, 42 (figure),
  43-44, 46-48

National Board for Professional
  Teaching Standards, xiv
National Council for the
  Accreditation of Teacher
  Education (NCATE), xiv
No Child Left Behind (NCLB) Act,
  26, 55, 66-67
Nurturing environment.
  See Classroom culture/climate

Organizational culture, 39-41

Pankake, A., 4
Parent conferences, 12
Parent-Teacher Association (PTA), 12
Peer tutoring, 57
Personal assessment, 91-93, 92
  (figure), 100-101, 109-110
Personal core values/moral code,
  28, 31-32
Personal enhancement model, 93-95,
  94 (figure)
Peters, T., 90
Physical disabilities, 69
Planning. *See* Action planning; Vision
Positive feedback, 3, 42
Preservice teachers:
  teacher leader role, perceptions
    of, 2-3
  teacher preparation programs
    and, 3
Proactive stance, 14, 17
Problem solving:
  critical analysis and, 5
  facilitator role and, 59
  systematic questioning approach
    and, 5
Problem-based learning:
  active/effective listening,
    82-83
  common ground, identification
    of/respect for, 70-71
  common vision of excellence,
    collaborative effort and, 73-74
  continuous enhancement, 103-104

developmentally appropriate instruction, 60-61

dropouts, teacher leadership and, 18-19

engaging/relevant curriculum, 59-60

ethics, established core values/moral code and, 29-31

fairness ethic, 32-34

in-depth personal assessment, 100-101

innovation, 48-49

integrity, personal core values/moral code and, 31-32

language, power to communicate, 83-84

learning expectations/appreciation/success, 45-46

learning/societal differences, acceptance/appreciation of, 71-72

ongoing systematic assessment, 61-62

professional demeanor, 34-35

public's right to know, 84-86

recreation/quiet needs, 101-103

respect/mutual trust, 46-48

vision, development/articulation of, 19-20

vision, implementation/stewardship of, 20-21

Professional associations, 99, 103

Professional demeanor, 29, 34-35, 77

Professional development, xiii, xiv
curriculum development and, 56
in-depth personal assessment and, 91-93, 92 (figure)
learning communities and, 11
partnerships and, 3
See also Teacher enhancement

Professional enhancement model, 93-95, 94 (figure)

Public's right to know, 81-82, 84-86, 109

Questioning strategy. See Systematic questioning approach

Quiet retreat, 95-98, 96 (figure), 101-102

Real-world curriculum, 57

Reciprocal determination cycle, 27 (figure), 28

Recreation, 95-98, 96 (figure), 101-102

Reflection, 95-98, 96 (figure), 101-102

Reflective inquiry, 5

Relevant curriculum, 55-56, 56 (figure), 59-60

Research-based change, 17

Resource recommendations:
communication skills, 118
curriculum/instruction, 115-117
equity for all learners, 117
ethics/integrity, 114-115
teacher enhancement, 118-120
vision, 113-114

Respect, 42 (figure), 43-44, 46-48, 67-68, 67 (figure), 109

Retirement, xiii

Right to know, 81-82, 84-86, 109

Risk taking, 3, 17, 44, 78

School improvement. See Systematic school improvement

Self-efficacy. See Student self-efficacy

Servant leadership model, 4-5

Societal differences, 68-69, 71-72, 108

Societal effects, 1, 10 (figure), 12-13, 16, 44, 110

Socratic method, 4-6, 11, 28, 109

Soul fatigue, 96-97

Staff development. See Professional development; Teacher enhancement

Stand-and-deliver instructional approach, 4

Standards, xiv, 27
Status quo, 4
Strodl, P., 2
Student performance, xiii, xiv
  high expectations and, 16
  learning communities and,
      11, 12-13
  student self-efficacy/confidence, 12
  teacher leadership and,
      2, 2 (figure)
  vision for achievement and,
      11, 14-15, 22
  See also Classroom culture/climate;
      Curriculum/instruction; Equity
      for all learners; Success in
      learning
Student self-efficacy, 12, 16
Study groups, 11
Success in learning, 42-43, 45-46,
      53, 110, 110 (figure)
Suranna, K. J., 2, 3
Systematic questioning approach,
      3, 5, 28
Systematic school improvement, xiv
  classroom culture/climate and,
      50-51
  communication skills and, 87
  curriculum/instruction and, 64
  equity for all learners and,
      75-76
  ethics/integrity, core values/moral
      code and, 37
  ideal-practice discrepancy and,
      3, 44-45
  learning communities and, 11
  teacher enhancement and,
      105-106
  vision, development/
      implementation of, 23
  See also Teacher leadership

Teacher enhancement, 5, 6, 12,
      89-90, 90 (figure), 104
  continuous enhancement, 91,
      98-100, 99 (figure), 103-104

in-depth personal assessment,
      91-93, 92 (figure),
      100-101
  personal/professional enhance-
      ment model, 93-95, 94 (figure)
  philosophical framework for,
      90-100
  problem-based learning and,
      100-104
  quiet/reflection/recreation needs,
      95-98, 96 (figure),
      101-102
  resource materials for, 118-120
  systematic school improvement
      and, 105-106
  See also Leadership development;
      Professional development
Teacher leadership, 2-4
  classroom context and, 1, 3
  group ethic/value system and, 2
  informal leadership roles, 2, 3
  leadership, definition of, 1, 3
  preservice teachers, perceptions of
      leadership and, 2-3
  servant leadership model and, 4-5
  skill development and, 1-2
  skills, conceptual framework for, 2
  Socratic approach and, 4-6, 11
  student performance and,
      2, 2 (figure)
  traits of teacher leaders, 3
  See also Leadership development;
      Learning communities;
      Professional development;
      Vision
Teacher preparation programs, 3
Teaching profession:
  stressors in, xiii
  teacher preparation programs
      and, 3
  See also Teacher leadership; Vision
Team processes, 11, 56
Truth, 5, 28, 109

Universal definitions, 5

Value systems. *See* Equity for all
    learners; Ethics/integrity
Vision, 4, 5, 10, 21-22, 107
    action plan for, 15-16, 15 (figure)
    common vision of excellence,
        69, 70 (figure), 73-74
    communication of, 12-13, 16,
        19-20
    consensus building models and, 14
    data-driven decision making and,
        14-15
    development of, 13-16, 19-20
    dropouts, teacher leadership and,
        18-19
    implementation/stewardship of,
        17, 20-21

improvement, proactive stance
    and, 14, 17
learning communities and,
    11-13
philosophical framework for, 10-11
planning phase and, 11, 13-14
problem-based learning and,
    18-21
resource materials for, 113-114
systematic school improvement
    and, 23
See also Ethics/integrity; Teacher
    leadership
Volunteers, 57

Wilmore, E., 93

CORWIN PRESS

The Corwin Press logo—a raven striding across an open book—represents the union of courage and learning. Corwin Press is committed to improving education for all learners by publishing books and other professional development resources for those serving the field of PreK–12 education. By providing practical, hands-on materials, Corwin Press continues to carry out the promise of its motto: **"Helping Educators Do Their Work Better."**